(1986)

IS IT REASONABLE
TO BELIEVE IN GOD?

IS IT REASONABLE TO BELIEVE IN GOD?

Edited and introduced by

J. HOUSTON

University of Glasgow

1984

The Handsel Press

Published by
The Handsel Press Ltd.
33 Montgomery Street, Edinburgh

ISBN 0 905312 13 9

First Published 1984

Printed in Great Britain by
Clark Constable, Edinburgh, London, Melbourne

CONTENTS

Contents

ACKNOWLEDGEMENTS

Grateful acknowledgement is due for the permission granted by the original publishers and authors of the papers collected in this volume, as follows:

Paper I, to Professor Swinburne; this paper has not previously been published in just this form.

Paper II, to Professor Flew and the Pemberton Publishing Company Limited; this paper originally appeared as a chapter of *The Presumption of Atheism*, London, 1976.

Paper III, to Professor Rowe and the editor of *The Monist*; this paper originally appeared in *The Monist*, Vol. 54, No. 3.

Paper IV, to Professor Swinburne and Cambridge University Press; this paper originally appeared in *Philosophy*, Vol. XLIII (No. 165).

Paper V, to Professor Horsburgh and the editor of *The Australasian Journal of Philosophy*, Vol. 35, No. 3.

Paper VI, to Professor Wainwright and the editor of *Ratio*; this paper originally appeared in *Ratio*, Vol. 15, No. 1.

Paper VII, to Professor Swinburne and Cambridge University Press; this paper originally appeared in Religious Studies, Vol. 4.

Paper VIII, to Professor Clark and The Aristotelian Society; this paper originally appeared in *The Proceedings of the Aristotelian Society*, 1977.

Paper IX, to Professor Stump and *The American Philosophical Quarterly*; this paper first appeared in *The American Philosophical Quarterly*, Vol. 16.

INTRODUCTION

In the quarter-century, from the end of the Second World War, philosophers of religion wrote a great deal about whether religious utterances, those apparently about God for instance, can be regarded as stating truths (or indeed falsehoods), or whether such utterances should perhaps be thought of as expressing emotion, articulating optional ways of regarding the world or of affirming and commending attitudes. Only utterances which are checkable (verifiable or falsifiable) against experience were supposed to be *factually* significant; and as it is unclear how what religious people say, for example about God, is empirically checkable, so it is inviting to attach to it a non-fact-stating significance.

In some theological circles this easily consorted with the view that objective truths are not of religious, or, as may be said, Christian, interest: religious faith is a way of relating to the objective world which the believer has (on some views he has it by a necessary choice; on others he finds that he has it), and not at all the acceptance of certain propositions as true. The believer's attitude to the world is complex, comprehensive, subtle, and is commended, expressed, evoked and prompted by writing and speech of many *genres*.

Well before the end of this period the failure of many ingenious and persistent attempts to formulate an acceptable empirical-checkability criterion for factual significance had widely undermined amongst philosophers the conviction that some such criterion exists. Possibly relatedly there was the influence of Philosophy of Science in which empirical testing came to be seen as a less important feature of the growth of scientific knowledge than had been supposed, so that by the late 1960s the connexion between empirical testability and scientific significance was at any rate much less clear than had earlier been thought.

Philosophers, to whom these developments were familiar, must now find much philosophy of religion which was published over the period I have sketched to be rather dated, and philosophy students coming now to philosophy of religion find some of that earlier work somewhat puzzling. One purpose of this volume is to make easily available some of the excellent and distinctively different philosophy of religion which has been published more recently.

Professor Flew's paper is most redolent of the earlier period; it challenges the legitimacy of our using a concept of God at all. But Flew mounts this challenge in a way which is less dependent on explicit empiricist criteria of meaningfulness than were the earlier challenges (amongst which his own challenges were prominent).

Several of the papers in the present volume are concerned with the force of particular arguments to show that God exists: the Cosmological argument, the argument from Design, arguments from religious experience. These papers could have been written (indeed one of them was) in the heyday of the empiricist challenge over the meaningfulness of religious language, accepting the legitimacy of the challenge, but trying to show that there are features of our experience which do support the assertion of God's existence (and so establish the factual significance of statements, as they must now be taken to be, about God). But effectively to defend a Cosmological or Teleological argument requires that certain well-known arguments of Hume be countered. One reason why the empiricist challenge over the meaningfulness of religious discourse was not earlier accepted and attempts made to meet it by appeal to Cosmological or Teleological arguments was the wide acceptance of these important Humean contentions, which have more recently been challenged, for example in two papers republished here. Rowe is concerned to rebut two very widely accepted, certainly broadly Humean arguments. Swinburne proposes an argument from Design which appeals to a different kind of order from that discussed by Hume, and not open to explanation in terms of evolutionary theory. Of necessity he devotes considerable attention to those several discussions in which Hume attacks any Teleological argument for the existence of God.

Religious experience has also been thought to give grounds for belief in God. Flew brings out some of the difficulties facing those who think so. The considerations brought to bear by Horsburgh (though he was not arguing specifically against Flew) constitute a particularly powerful, unjustly neglected statement of the case. Experience of what is known as the physical world and experience of what is claimed to be a religious reality can best be argued to be analogous, in order to establish objectivity for what is religiously experienced, if what is experienced religiously is the topic of inter-personal discourse, the more complex and determinate the better, and is found to have some predictability. Thus if arguments from religious experience are rationally to confirm belief in God's existence, an investigation, more than philosophical, of the communications and experience of mystics and other recipients of religious experience (perhaps most believers) will be required. But it is philosophical enquiry which establishes what is required and why. Wainwright contends that the existence of an adequate scientific explanation of religious experience does not call for a denial that the experiences are experiences of an objective religious reality.

In the first of his papers included here, Swinburne succinctly dis-tinguishes different sorts of arguments which might be offered for the existence of God, and gives reasons for holding that such arguments ought to be considered together if the overall probability of God's existence is to be rationally assessed. Whether we act on this advice will depend (of course) on what we think of it, and also what force, if any, we think arguments for the existence of God have. But it is a mark of recent philosophy of religion that it allows the possibility or investigates the force of what is often called a cumulative case for theism.

Adopting a religious belief, so far as this is *possible*, by deliberate choice, might be a rational prudent policy, even though it is judged to be more probable than not that the belief is false, if for instance there are very drastic consequences for our felicity in rejecting a particular belief if it turns out to be true, and no comparable risks in accepting it if it turns out to be false. In *The Christian* Wager, Swinburne explores this line of reasoning.

Atheists have had no difficulty in identifying evils in the world which, they think, rule out reasonable belief in the existence of an omnicompetent benevolent god. Clark's paper is a distinctive dis-cussion of this issue, *inter alia* because he not only explores fairly standard attempts to reconcile divine sovereignty and the pains and injustices of the world, but he also seeks out the implications for our world-view of *our making* these evaluations which we take to be objec-tive, of the world as full of evil and injustice, and the implications of our making all the judgements which we make as being *true*. Clark contends that we have a *choice*, which of its nature cannot itself be rational, between, on the one hand, moral seriousness including care for rationality and truth, which stance cannot be consistently atheistic, and on the other, whatever attitude towards our experience it pleases us to adopt. So while we cannot rationally establish theism, our perception of evils in the world *as* evils undermines rational humanism also, and does not rationally entitle us to affirm atheism. The point in this connexion of much Gnostic and Christian thought is brought out by Clark's method of presentation which both uses and illuminates the History of Ideas. At the same time, the very modern debates over the autonomy of ethics, and between holders of realist and anti-realist views of truth are shown to relate importantly to the paper's concern.

Believing in God involves trust, as well as believing that God exists. (A so-called "trust in God" which does *not* involve belief that God exists has its place in the sort of theology, sketched in the second paragraph above, in which having faith is having an attitude to the world involving will and emotions.) One way in which trust in God is most commonly shown, is by the believer's making requests of him. But if God is all-powerful, all-knowing and all-loving, is there any point in petitionary prayer? Won't such a god do what's best without our asking; and won't he refuse our prayer if what we ask is less than the best? This question is addressed by Stump's paper.

These last three papers presuppose, without mentioning it, that it *is* factually meaningful to talk about God. That intellectual energy can, with a good conscience, be devoted to the topics of these papers without raising that issue betokens change of the kind I have mentioned in philosophy of religion.

This collection, therefore, consists of papers typifying the high standard to be found in much recent writing in philosophy of religion, papers marking clear changes in climate in that sphere, and above all offering penetrating discussions of their subjects. It is published to make this work more readily accessible to, and known by, people with philosophical or theological interests (insofar as the theology which claims no knowledge is based on the belief that no defensible alternative exists, some of these papers will serve usefully to call it in question). Some of the papers will be found, by readers quite new to these issues, to be more straight-forward than others: I judge *Arguments for the Existence of God, The Argument from Design,* and *Petitionary Prayer* to be most easily understood, while *God, Good and Evil* due to its wide range requires (and rewards) most work from the reader.

Paper I
Introductory Groundwork

'Believing in God' often means more than 'believing that God exists'; so loving, obeying, trusting, and worshipping God may also be involved, and most believers in God would say that the belief in God's existence is not alone sufficient for faith proper. But belief in God's existence is, surely, necessary for any belief in God.[1] Since, in addition, it has seemed to many people particularly difficult to justify belief in God's existence[2] those concerned about the rationality of belief in God have often discussed the rationality of belief in the existence of God: 'Show me that your God exists, and I may then take your religious faith more seriously' is the kind of challenge often posed, both by the faithful, concerned to establish grounds for their belief, and by the unbeliever.

In order to respond to the challenge, and before examining particular arguments, and grounds which have been offered, it is worth considering what should count as *showing* that God exists. Arguments, which set out the support given to their conclusions by their premises, are frequently characterised as deductive or inductive. In a valid deductive argument it is quite impossible for the premise(s) to be true unless the conclusion is also true: the premise(s) constitute(s) conclusive support for the conclusion, so that given the truth of the argument's premise(s), the conclusion, in being reached by valid inference, is beyond rational doubt. Theorems in school geometry, such as that associated with the name of Pythagoras, afford examples of deductive reasoning.

Inductive reasoning lays no claim to conclusiveness for its conclusions, in relation to, and as supported by, the premise(s) presented. Nevertheless, while, in inductive argument it is recognised that where the premise(s) are true and the argument properly constructed, the conclusion may in fact be false, yet the premise(s) are shown to give some support to the conclusion. Argument in support of scientific hypotheses, like Boyle's law, offers a stock example of inductive reasoning.

Sometimes the request to be *shown* that God exists is intended as a request for a deductive argument, with indubitably true premises which validly concludes that God exists. Only such an argument will establish God's existence with *certainty*, or so it has been widely held. Nothing less than certainty will suffice over this issue, it is thought, perhaps because in a matter as important as our eternal destiny we must have complete assurance, or perhaps (less creditably) because we will not yield self-pleasing autonomy unless it is quite certain that we must. Perhaps it is thought that a belief which is less than certain should only be held with reservations, tentatively, and that this is inappropriate to belief in God. However, since we can make mistakes in constructing or evaluating deductive arguments, engaging in what aspires to be valid deduction does not guarantee success, and therefore does not secure certainty for conclusions reached – and this even where premises are known for certain. Whether certainty is desirable or attainable, the mere fact of engaging in *deductive* argument will not secure it.

Inductive reasoning makes no claim to provide certainty, and so believers who have insisted that belief in God must be unreserved, wholeheartedly committed, have concluded that belief in God cannot be dependent on any kind of argument, and must indeed be held independently of any such rational support as argument can provide.[3] Such a view is often called Fideism.

Seldom, if ever, is a whole case for theism solely deductive. Sometimes a cosmological argument is presented on its own, apparently as a deductive argument for the existence of God, but the appearance can deceive. Sometimes a premise is inductively supported, and sometimes the argument, with its conclusion, is brought together with other arguments to form part of a 'cumulative case' for theism.[4] Much the best known deductive argument for God's existence is the so-called Ontological argument, the sustained and often subtle controversy over which well illustrates the remark above that the employment of deductive procedures does not secure certainty. In Anselm's version of the argument, God is understood to be 'that than which nothing greater can be thought'. In this, 'great' is an evaluative word, rather than a word connoting mere size; and the later formulation of Descartes, who takes God to be 'the being who has all perfections' serves to make this point clearer to us. Now, if it is better to have existence than not to exist, if existence is a perfection, then the greatest, or most perfect being must have it, must exist. So runs this deductive argument for

2

the existence of God, raising persisting questions over whether by analogous reasoning we should affirm the existence of the most perfect conceivable island, and whether existence is a perfection, or indeed a property at all. Further, to think of God as '*that* than which none greater can be thought' or as '*the* most perfect conceivable being' appears to assume without support that there is only *one* being as great as can be thought, only a single being possessing all perfections. A conviction of monotheists appears to be covertly imported without obvious justification; but a formulation of the argument which excludes this assumption, and says only that a being which, anything which, has all perfections must exist (or that a being, anything, than which none greater can be conceived must exist) at best establishes that *a* god exists. And even that best is a doubtful best. If this formulation means 'anything which has all perfections must exist', the question *remains* of whether there is any such thing. If it means 'there necessarily is a being which has all perfections', this *might* appear to follow from conceiving of a being, supposed to have all perfections, and reflecting that if it truly *has* all perfections, then *it* must exist. Well, perhaps something which really exists having all perfections, *must* exist, but it is not clear that 'some thing' (having all perfections) which is only conceived of, suppositious, must exist.

Inductive argument for the existence of God is the principal concern of the following paper. In large part this is because, as we have seen, deductive argument to God's existence is patently fraught with difficulty. But also, the nature of inductive argument itself, (and, indeed, even its acceptability) has been extensively questioned. Professor Swinburne has contributed to this wider discussion; and in the present paper he briefly considers inductive argumentation to the existence of God.[5]

NOTES

1. Christian scripture suggests as much, at Hebrews 11, 6.
2. Compare a worry like 'Is it rational for me to court Mary?' where the question of the very existence of Mary, not being open to doubt, will not be (any part of) what concerns us, and questions about Mary's availability, feelings, character and disposition will be likelier ones to pursue.
3. For perceptive discussion of this view, see e.g. B. Mitchell, *The Justification of Religious Belief.* London, 1973. Part III, pp. 99 ff.
4. For Professor Swinburne's much fuller discussion of such a case, see his *The Existence of God.* Oxford, 1979. See also B. Mitchell, op. cit. ch. 3.
5. His later paper (pp. 53 ff. below) to which he refers at his note 2, sets out one such argument, a form of argument from design.

3

Arguments for the Existence of God[1]

R. G. SWINBURNE

In the course of human history many men have taken for granted the existence of God, and many others have taken for granted his non-existence. They have not had consciously formulated reasons for their beliefs. They have just believed. However, others who have believed have had reasons for their beliefs. As with most men's reasons for most of their beliefs, these reasons have often been very vague and incohate. Yet sometimes men have formulated some of their reasons for belief in a sharp and explicit form. Then we have something clearly recognisable as an argument for or against the existence of God. Those arguments which have been frequently discussed have been given names – and thus we have 'the cosmological argument', or 'the argument from religious experience'. However, other arguments exist which have not been discussed frequently enough to gain a name, and men have had other reasons for belief or disbelief which have never been formulated explicitly enough to constitute an argument. In this short paper I wish to make some general points about the nature of arguments for or against the existence of God.

An argument starts from one or more premises and argues to a conclusion. An argument is deductively valid if it is incoherent to suppose that its premises are true but its conclusion false. Among arguments which are not deductively valid there are arguments in which the premises in some sense 'support' or 'confirm' or 'give strength to' the conclusion, and some or all arguments of this general kind are often characterised as 'good' or 'correct' or 'strong' inductive arguments. However we need here to distinguish carefully between two different kinds of argument. There are arguments in which the premises make the conclusion probable, that is more probable than not – e.g.

4

P_1: 70% inhabitants of the Bogside are Catholic
P_2: Docherty is an inhabitant of the Bogside
C: Docherty is Catholic

The conjunction of the premises makes the conclusion probable. However, many arguments which are called 'correct' inductive arguments are hardly to be regarded as of this type. Take a typical enumerative argument:

P: all of 1000 ravens observed in different parts of the world are black.

C: all ravens are black.

The normal way to construe the conclusion, in the context of a discussion of inductive arguments, is to suppose that it is about all ravens at all moments of time and points of space – and, even if you suppose that nothing on a distant planet would count as a raven, that means all ravens at all times in the Earth's history and at all places on its surface. But, when the conclusion is interpreted this way it becomes implausible to suppose that P makes C more probable than not. For it is not unreasonable to suppose that the blackness of observed ravens arises from a particular feature of modern ravens, a particular feature of their genotype not present in older ravens. Maybe, despite P, there was somewhere just one non-black raven. Certainly P *adds* to the probability of C and so, on some technical definitions of 'confirm', confirms C, but it does not make it probable. The same point can be made with greater force with respect to a typical scientific argument from various data of observation and experiment to conclusions about what are the laws of nature. Laws of nature are normally supposed to be generalisations which not merely hold at all times and places, but would continue to hold under unrealised or unrealisable circumstances. Here too we may indeed admit that the various observations made by Tycho Brahe, Kepler, and Galileo and other men of the seventeenth century made it more likely, more probable, that Newton's theory was true than it would have been without them. But it seems an exaggeration to say that they made it more probable than not. For it would have not been unreasonable to suppose that Newton's laws hold only because of some pervasive feature of our spatio-temporal region and so do not apply universally.

Let us call an argument in which the premises make the conclusion probable a correct P-inductive argument. Let us call an argument in which the premises add to the probability of the conclusion a

5

correct C-inductive argument. (Here, in the technical sense often used, we may say that the premisses 'confirm' the conclusion). Among correct C-inductive arguments some will obviously be stronger than others, in the sense that in some the premisses will raise the probability of the conclusion more than the premisses do in other arguments. Now the point of an argument is to get people, in so far as they are rational, to accept the conclusion. For this purpose it is not sufficient that the premisses should in some sense necessitate or probabilify the conclusion. It is also necessary that the premisses should be known to be true by those who dispute about the conclusion. There are plenty of valid arguments to the existence of God which are quite useless, because although their premisses may be true, they are not known to be true by men who argue about religion – e.g.

P_1: If coal is black, God exists.
P_2: coal is black
C: God exists.

What are clearly of interest to men in an age of religious scepticism are arguments to the existence (or non-existence) of God in which the premisses are known to be true by men of all theistic or atheistic persuasions. I therefore define arguments from premisses known to be true by those who dispute about the conclusion, which are valid deductive, correct P-inductive, or correct C-inductive arguments, respectively good deductive, good P-inductive and good C-inductive arguments. In investigating arguments for or against the existence of god, we need to see if any of them are of any of these latter kinds.

Almost all the arguments for or against the existence of God start from premisses known to be true by men of all theistic or atheistic persuasions. What is at stake is how much force they give to their conclusion. The ontological argument is clearly intended to be a valid deductive argument, and it is hard to see how it could be construed as an inductive argument. However, the ontological argument seems to me very much on its own. Most other arguments to the existence of God seem to be construable as inductive arguments, even though some of their proponents may have intended them to be regarded as deductive arguments. They are arguments of a pattern common in science, history, and other fields – arguments to the best explanation of the phenomena described by the premisses. The scientist argues from various phenomena, say positions of planets or readings of instruments in the laboratory, to some theory which explains those phenomena –

to a theory about how planets always move, or to a theory about observed substances being made of millions of molecules. The historian argues from various archaeological remains to a Roman detachment having lived on the site for two hundred years. Likewise the detective argues from clues to something which explains the clues. In these cases the phenomena make the theory probable (i.e. make it probable that the theory gives the true explanation of those phenomena) in so far as (1) the theory is a simple one, and (2) the phenomena are ones which you would expect to find if the theory were true.

The cosmological argument, the argument from design, the argument from religious experience, and arguments from miracles and history seem to me to have this structure. The cosmological argument starts from the evident datum of experience that there is a world, and claims that this is something which needs explaining and is best explained by supposing that God made it and keeps it in existence. The argument from design starts from the fact that the world is an orderly one and claims that this is best explained by the action of God who keeps it thus. What the orderliness of the world consists in, of course, needs spelling out – I myself think that the most evident facet of its orderliness is the fact that things behave in the regular way described by scientific laws. The argument from design then claims that their regular operation is to be explained by God who keeps them going.[2]

Other arguments to the existence of God argue from more specific features of the world – various experiences of religious men, the history of civilisation, the reports recorded in the New Testament of the life, death and resurrection of Jesus, the history of the Church etc. etc. In the case of each argument we need to assess whether it is a good P-inductive or a good C-inductive argument to the existence of God.

One unfortunate feature of recent philosophy of religion is the tendency to treat arguments for (and against) the existence of God in isolation from each other. There can, of course, be no objection to considering each argument initially, as I have just done, for the sake of simplicity of exposition, in isolation from others. But clearly the arguments may back each other up or alternatively weaken each other, and we need to consider whether or not they do. Some very misguided philosophers consider the arguments for the existence of God one by one, saying: the cosmological argument does not prove its conclusion, the teleological argument does not etc. etc., therefore the arguments do not prove their conclusion. This 'divide and rule' technique with the arguments is inadmissible. Even if the only kind of good argument was a valid deductive argument (from premisses known to be true), it would be inadmissible. An argument from p to r may be invalid; another argument from q to r may be invalid. But if you run the arguments together, you could well get a valid deductive argument; the argument from p and q to r may indeed be valid. The argument from 'all students have long hair' to 'Smith has long hair' is invalid, and so is the argument from 'Smith is a student' to 'Smith has long hair'; but the argument from 'all students have long hair and Smith is a student' to 'Smith has long hair' is valid.

That arguments may support and weaken each other is even more evident, when we are dealing with inductive arguments. That Smith has blood on his hands hardly makes it probable that Smith murdered Mrs. Jones, nor (by itself) does the fact that Smith stood to gain from Mrs. Jones' death, nor (by itself) does the fact that Smith was near the scene of the murder at the time of its being committed, but together (perhaps with other data) they do indeed make the conclusion probable.

So it is important after we have considered the arguments separately, to consider their cumulative effect. It may well be for example that none of the arguments for the existence of God taken separately are good P-inductive arguments, but that many of them are good C-inductive arguments, and perhaps that all of them together form a good P-inductive argument. Arguments against the existence of God, such as the argument from evil, must also be taken into account. Even if the argument from evil to the non-existence of God is not a good deductive argument it may have considerable inductive force. The really interesting question is whether an argument from all relevant considerations, counting for or against the existence of God, makes the existence of God more probable than not. Whether this is so, and whether the particular arguments are good P-inductive or good C-inductive arguments is something which we can only settle when we have got clear about the criteria for arguments being good P- or C-inductive arguments. To get clear about this we need to examine carefully the grounds on which we judge, in other less controversial fields such as history and science, that claims are probable or are confirmed by evidence. Whether the arguments for or against the existence of

God 'work' is a more complicated matter than some philosophers of religion have led us to believe. There are no easy knock-down answers to be had here.

NOTES

1. This paper is based on the opening lecture of my Wilde Lectures for 1975/6, delivered in the University of Oxford in the Hilary Term 1976.
2. I discuss this way of understanding the argument from design in my paper 'The Argument from Design' included in the present collection, pp. 53-67, and first published in *Philosophy* 1968, Vol. 43, pp. 199-212.

QUESTIONS for further discussion:

1. In inductive arguments *do* premises really give support to the conclusions which they are supposed to support? For example, do premises such as 'Raven 1 is black', 'Raven 2 is black', ... 'Raven n is black', give grounds for believing the conclusion 'All ravens are black'? If not, what other fields of enquiry, besides that to which the present book relates, will be affected, and how?
2. Is Swinburne *quite* fair in saying that the divide-and-rule technique, which he gives his reasons for rejecting as applied to inductive argument, is inapplicable even where exclusively deductive argument is concerned? Is 'running two invalid deductive arguments together' a tendentious way of describing the construction of what is a completely new argument, rather than an argument composed of other arguments? (May it better be described as 'composed of *components* of other arguments'?)

Paper II
Introductory Groundwork

In asking whether God exists we must suppose ourselves to have a conception of God. It need not be a conception which is in every respect determinate, and *some* unresolved controversy about its content (such as that about God's immutability mentioned below) can be set aside when we raise the issue of God's existence. However, Professor Flew holds that we cannot, and should not uncritically, without good reason (which we must provide), suppose that there is concept of God which is employable.

If central features of our proposed concept are logically incompatible then this concept cannot be applied to anything. So, for example, immutability has been thought incompatible with knowledge of a changing world (requiring changes in God's knowledge) or with loving (requiring emotions which are at least possibly changeable).[1]

And even if there be no question of *internal* incoherence, questions can be raised over whether a concept ever could, even in principle, be applied in the world we know. This is not merely the question of whether there exists something to which the concept does apply, but whether there could, even theoretically-possibly, be conditions in which the concept can justifiably be employed. It would be a mistake, of course, to regard this question, though it has a certain logical priority, as requiring to be settled before we consider arguments for the existence of God. Indeed one way of showing that our concept of God has possible application will be to establish that it has actual application by establishing that some argument for the existence of God has some force. Consequently the full discussion, which constitutes Flew's most recent challenge to the theist, must appraise the arguments offered for God's existence. The present paper which is the first chapter of Flew's book of the same title gives a full sketch of this challenge, indicating the further phases of the book's full length treatment. It serves as an agenda, with commentary, for Flew's discussion, and can set the contents of this volume in a particular perspective which it is important to consider.

An appeal to religious experience as a possible justification for the use of the concept 'god' is challenged by asking whether religious experience really is like perception of the physical world, giving grounds for claims to knowledge of what is 'perceived'. In the course of this, Flew's allusion to difficulties for those who maintain that all we ever directly see is visual sense-data, has in mind, for example, the difficulty of how, if all we immediately see are visual sense-data, we can have grounds for thinking that these subjective experiences are caused by, or correspond to, anything independent of us, which *ex hypothesi* we never directly experience.

If no argument for God's existence has any force, the question whether 'god' could have application calls for investigation into conditions for meaning in general, a topic of continuing urgent discussion in modern philosophy.[2]

NOTES

1. For discussion of the logical coherence of concepts of God, see e.g. Professor Swinburne's *The Coherence of Theism.* Oxford, 1977; also A. Kenny, *The God of the Philosophers.* Oxford, 1979.
2. For a survey of earlier discussion see A. Plantinga, *God and Other Minds.* Cornell, 1967. Ch. 7. Plantinga's conclusions were unfavourable to Flew. For a reply, see K. Nielsen, *Contemporary Critiques of Religion.* London, 1971, pp. 55 ff.

The Presumption of Atheism

A. FLEW

1. *What it is, and why it matters*

At the beginning of Book X of his last work *The Laws,* Plato turns his attention from violent and outrageous actions in general to the particular case of undisciplined and presumptuous behaviour in matters of religion:

> We have already stated summarily what the punishment should be for temple-robbing, whether by open force or secretly. But the punishments for the various sorts of insolence in speech or action with regard to the gods, which a man can show in word or deed, have to be proclaimed after we have provided an exordium. Let this be it: 'No one believing, as the laws prescribe, in the existence of the gods has ever yet performed an impious action willingly, or uttered a lawless word. Anyone acting in such a way is in one of three conditions: either, first, he does not believe the proposition aforesaid; or, second, he believes that though the gods exist they have no concern about men; or, third, he believes that they can easily be won over by the bribery of prayer and sacrifice' (§885B).[1]

So Plato in his notorious treatment of heresy might be said to be rebuking the presumption of atheism. The word 'presumption' would then be employed as a synonym for 'presumptuousness'. But, despite the interest of the questions raised by Plato, the term has in my title a different interpretation. The presumption of atheism which I want to discuss is not a form of presumptuousness. Indeed it might be regarded as an expression of the very opposite, a modest teachability. My presumption of atheism is closely analogous to the presumption of innocence in the English law; a comparison which I shall develop in Section 2. What I want to examine is the contention that the debate about the existence of God should properly begin from the presumption of atheism, that the onus of proof must lie upon the theist.

The word 'atheism', however, has in this contention to be construed unusually. Whereas nowadays the usual meaning of 'atheist' in English is 'someone who asserts that there is no such being as God', I want the word to be understood not positively but negatively. I want the originally Greek prefix 'a' to be read in the same way in 'atheist' as it customarily is read in such other Greco-English words as 'amoral', 'atypical', and 'asymmetrical'. In this interpretation an atheist becomes: not someone who positively asserts the non-existence of God; but someone who is simply not a theist. Let us, for future ready reference, introduce the labels 'positive atheist' for the former and 'negative atheist' for the latter.

The introduction of this new interpretation of the word 'atheism' may appear to be a piece of perverse Humpty-Dumptyism, going arbitrarily against established common usage.[2] 'Whyever', it could be asked, 'don't you make it not the presumption of atheism but the presumption of agnosticism?' It is too soon to attempt a full answer to this challenge and this suggestion. My justification for introducing the notion of negative atheism will be found in the whole development of the present chapter. Then in Chapter Two I intend to argue for a return to the original usage of the word 'agnosticism', as first introduced by Thomas Henry Huxley. In the meantime it should be sufficient to point out that, following the present degenerate usage, an agnostic is one who, having entertained the proposition that God exists, now claims not to know either that it is or that it is not true. To be in this ordinary sense an agnostic you have already to have conceded that there is, and that you have, a legitimate concept of God; such that, whether or not this concept does in fact have application, it theoretically could. But the atheist in my peculiar interpretation, unlike the atheist in the usual sense, has not as yet and as such conceded even this.

This point is important, though the question whether the word 'agnosticism' could bear the meaning which I want now to give to the word 'atheism' is not. What the protagonist of my presumption of atheism wants to show is that the debate about the existence of God ought to be conducted in a particular way, and that the issue should be seen in a certain perspective. His thesis about the onus of proof involves that it is up to the theist: first, to introduce and to defend his proposed concept of God; and, second, to provide sufficient reason for believing that this concept of his does in fact have an application.

It is the first of these two stages which needs perhaps to be emphasised even more strongly than the second. Where the question of existence concerns, for instance, a Loch Ness Monster or an Abominable Snowman, this stage may perhaps reasonably be deemed to be more or less complete before the argument begins. But in the controversy about the existence of God this is certainly not so: not only for the quite familiar reason that the word 'God' is used – or misused – in many different ways; but also, and much more interestingly, because it cannot be taken for granted that even the would-be mainstream theist is operating with a legitimate concept which theoretically could have an application to an actual being.

This last suggestion is not really as new-fangled and factitious as it is sometimes thought to be. But its pedigree has been made a little hard to trace. For the fact is that, traditionally, issues which should be seen as concerning the legitimacy or otherwise of a proposed or supposed concept have by philosophical theologians been discussed, either as surely disposable difficulties in reconciling one particular feature of the Divine nature with another, or else as aspects of an equally surely soluble general problem of saying something about the infinite Creator in language intelligible to His finite creatures. These traditional and still almost universally accepted forms of presentation are fundamentally prejudicial. For they assume that there is a Divine Being, with an actual nature the features of which we can investigate. They assume that there is an Infinite Creator, whose existence – whatever difficulties we finite creatures may have in asserting anything else about Him – we may take for granted.

The general reason why this presumption of atheism matters is that its acceptance must put the whole question of the existence of God into an entirely fresh perspective. Most immediately relevant here is that in this fresh perspective problems which really are conceptual are seen as conceptual problems; and problems which have tended to be regarded as advanced and, so to speak, optional extras now discover themselves as both elementary and indispensable. The theist who wants to build a systematic and thorough apologetic finds that he is required to begin absolutely from the beginning. This absolute beginning is to ensure that the word 'God' is provided with a meaning such that it is theoretically possible for an actual being to be so described.

Although I shall later be arguing that the presumption of atheism is neutral as between all parties to the main dispute, in as much as to accept it as determining a procedural framework is not to make any substantive assumptions, I must give fair warning now that I do nevertheless believe that in its fresh perspective the whole enterprise of theism appears even more difficult and precarious than it did before. In part this is a corollary of what I have just been suggesting: that certain difficulties and objections, which may previously have seemed peripheral or even factitious, are made to stand out as fundamental and unavoidable. But it is also in part, as we shall be seeing soon, a consequence of the emphasis which it places on the imperative need to produce some sort of sufficient reason to justify theist belief.

2. *The presumption of atheism and the presumption of innocence*

One thing which helps to conceal this need is a confusion about the possible varieties of proof, and this confusion is one which can be resolved with the help of the first of a series of comparisons between my proposed presumption of atheism and the legal presumption of innocence.

(i) It is frequently said nowadays, even by professing Roman Catholics, that everyone knows that it is impossible to prove the existence of God. The first objection to this putative truism is, as my reference to Roman Catholics should have suggested, that it is not true. For it is an essential dogma of Roman Catholicism, defined as such by the First Vatican Council, that 'the one and true God our creator and lord can be known for certain through the creation by the natural light of human reason' (Denzinger, §1806). So even if this dogma is, as I myself believe, false, it is certainly not known to be false by those many Roman Catholics who remain, despite all the disturbances consequent upon the Second Vatican Council, committed to the complete traditional faith.

To this a sophisticated objector might reply that the definition of the First Vatican Council speaks of knowing for certain rather than of proving or demonstrating; adding perhaps, if he was very sophisticated indeed, that the word 'demonstrari' in an earlier draft was eventually replaced by the expression 'certo cognosci'. But, allowing that this is correct, it is certainly not enough to vindicate the conventional wisdom. For the word 'proof' is not ordinarily restricted in its application to demonstratively valid arguments, that is, in which the conclusion cannot be denied without thereby contradicting the premises. So it is too flattering to suggest that most of those who make this facile claim, that everyone knows that it is impossible to prove the existence of God, are intending only the strictly limited assertion that one special sort of proof, demonstrative proof, is impossible.

The truth, and the danger, is that wherever there is any awareness of such a limited and specialised interpretation, there will be a quick and illegitimate move to the much wider general conclusion that it is impossible and, furthermore, unnecessary to provide any sufficient reason for believing. It is, therefore, worth underlining that when the presumption of atheism is explained as insisting that the onus of proof must be on the theist, the word 'proof' is being used in the ordinary wide sense in which it can embrace any and every variety of sufficient reason. It is, of course, in this and only this sense that the word is interpreted when the presumption of innocence is explained as laying the onus of proof on the prosecution.

(ii) A second element of positive analogy between these two presumptions is that both are defeasible; and that they are, consequently, not to be identified with assumptions. The presumption of innocence indicates where the court should start and how it must proceed. Yet the prosecution is still able, more often than not, to bring forward what is in the end accepted as sufficient reason to warrant the verdict 'Guilty'; which appropriate sufficient reason is properly characterised as a proof of guilt. The defeasible presumption of innocence is thus in this majority of cases in fact defeated. Were the indefeasible innocence of all accused persons an assumption of any legal system, then there could not be within that system any provision for any verdict other than 'Not Guilty'. To the extent that it is, for instance, an assumption of the English Common Law that every citizen is cognisant of all that the law requires of him, that law cannot admit the fact that this assumption is, as in fact it is, false.

The presumption of atheism is similarly defeasible. It lays it down that thorough and systematic inquiry must start from a position of negative atheism, and that the burden of proof lies on the theist proposition. Yet this is not at all the same thing as demanding that the debate should proceed on either a positive or a negative atheist assumption, which must preclude a theist conclusion. Counsel for theism no more betrays his client by accepting the framework determined by this presumption than counsel for the prosecution betrays the state by conceding the legal presumption of innocence. The latter is perhaps in his heart unshakably convinced of the guilt of the defendant. Yet he must, and with complete consistency and perfect sincerity may, insist that the proceedings of the court should respect the presumption of innocence. The former is even more likely to be persuaded of the soundness of his brief. Yet he too can with a good conscience allow that a thorough and complete apologetic must start from, meet, and go on to defeat, the presumption of atheism.

Put as I have just been putting it, the crucial distinction between a defeasible presumption and a categorical assumption will, no doubt, seem quite obvious. But obviousness really is, what some other things nowadays frequently said to be are not, essentially relative: what is obvious to one person at one time may not have been obvious to that same person at an earlier time, and may not be obvious now to another. There is no doubt but that many do find the present distinction difficult to grasp, especially in its application to exciting cases. Indeed one reason why I decided to write the lecture on which the present chapter is based is that I had found even the most acute and sympathetic critics of my *God and Philosophy* faulting me for asking everyone to start from my own notoriously atheist assumptions. It was clear that a more lucid and more adequately argued statement was needed. For in that book I had recommended only the present methodological presumption, not a substantive assumption.

I cite another example from a quite different sphere, an example which is again the more salutary since the offender was above suspicion of any dishonourable intent wilfully to misunderstand or misrepresent. Lord Attlee, once Leader of the British Labour Party, reproached the 'general assumption that all applicants are frauds unless they prove themselves otherwise'. But, we must insist, to put the onus of proof of entitlement upon the beneficiary is not to assume that all, or most, or even any of those who apply for welfare benefits are in fact cheats. Such presumptions are procedural purely. They assume no substantive conclusions.

(iii) However – and here we come to a third element in the positive analogy – to say that such presumptions are in themselves procedural and not substantive is not to say that the higher-order questions of whether to follow this presumption or that are trifling and merely formal rather than material and substantial. These higher-order questions are not questions which can be dismissed cynically as 'issues of principle as opposed to issues of substance'. It can matter a lot which presumption is adopted. Notoriously there is a world of difference between legal systems which follow the presumption of innocence, and those which do not. And, as I began to indicate at the end of Section 1, to adopt the presumption of atheism does put the whole argument into a distinctive perspective.

(iv) Next, as a fourth element in the positive analogy, it is a paradoxical consequence of the fact that these presumptions are procedural and not substantive that particular defeats do not constitute any sort of reason, much less a sufficient reason, for a general surrender. The fact that George Joseph Smith was in his trial proved guilty of many murders defeats the original presumption of his innocence. But this particular defeat has no tendency at all to show that even in this particular case the court should not have proceeded on this presumption. Still less does it tend to establish that the legal system as a whole was at fault in incorporating this presumption as a general principle. It is the same with the presumption of atheism. Suppose that someone is able to prove the existence of God. This achievement must, similarly, defeat our presumption. But it does not thereby show that the original contention about the onus of proof was mistaken.

Etymologically the word 'defeasible' (=defeatable) does imply precisely this capacity to survive defeat. A substantive generalisation – such as, for instance, the assertion that all persons accused of murder are in fact innocent – is falsified decisively by the production of even one authentic counter-example. But a defeasible presumption is not shown to have been the wrong one to have made by being in a particular case in fact defeated.

3. *The case for the presumption of atheism*

What does show the presumption of atheism to be the right one is what we have now to investigate.

(i) An obvious first move is to appeal to the old legal axiom: 'Ei incumbit probatio qui dicit, non qui negat.' Literally and unsympathetically translated this becomes: 'The onus of proof lies on the man who affirms, not on the man who denies.' To this an objection is almost equally obvious. Given just a very little verbal ingenuity, the content of any motion can be rendered alternatively in either a negative or a positive form: either, 'That this house affirms the existence of God'; or, 'That this house takes its stand for atheism'. So interpreted, therefore, our axiom provides no determinate guidance.[3]

Suppose, however, that we take the hint already offered in the previous paragraph. A less literal but more sympathetic translation would be: 'The onus of proof lies on the proposition, not on the opposition.' The point of the change is to bring out that this maxim was offered in a legal context, and that our courts are institutions of debate. An axiom providing no determinate guidance outside that framework may nevertheless be fundamental for the effective conduct of orderly and decisive debate. Here the outcome is supposed to be decided on the merits of what is said within the debate itself, and of that alone. So no opposition can set about demolishing the proposition case until and unless that proposition has first provided them with a case for demolition: 'You've got to get something on your plate before you can start messing it around' (J. L. Austin).

Of course our maxim even when thus sympathetically interpreted still offers no direction which contending parties ought to be made to undertake which roles. Granting that courts are to operate as debating institutions, and granting that this maxim is fundamental to debate, we have to appeal to some further premise principle before we become licensed to infer that the prosecution must propose and the defence oppose. This further principle is, once again, the familiar presumption of innocence. Were we, while retaining the conception of a court as an institution for reaching decisions by way of formalised debate, to embrace the opposite presumption, the presumption of guilt, we should need to adopt the opposite arrangements. In these the defence would first propose that the accused is after all innocent, and the prosecution would then respond by struggling to disintegrate the case proposed.

(ii) The first move examined cannot, therefore, be by itself sufficient. To have considered it does nevertheless help to show that to accept such a presumption is to adopt a policy. And policies have to be assessed by reference to the aims of those for whom they are suggested. If for you it is more important that no guilty person should ever be acquitted than that no innocent person should ever be convicted, then for you a presumption of guilt must be the rational policy. For you, with your preference structure, a presumption of innocence becomes simply irrational. To adopt this policy would be to adopt means calculated to frustrate your own chosen ends; which is, surely, paradigmatically irrational. Take, as an actual illustration, the controlling elite of a ruling Leninist party, which must as such refuse to recognise any individual rights if these conflict with the claims of the party, and which in fact treats all those suspected of actual or potential opposition much as if they were already known 'counter-revolutionaries', 'enemies of socialism', 'friends of the United States', 'advocates of free elections', and all other like things bad. I can, and do, fault this policy and its agents on many counts. Yet I cannot say that for them, once granted their scale of values, it is irrational.

What then are the aims by reference to which an atheist presumption might be justified? One key word in the answer, if not the key word, must be 'knowledge'. The context for which such a policy is proposed is that of inquiry about the existence of God; and the object of the exercise is, presumably, to discover whether it is possible to establish that the word 'God' does in fact have application. Now to establish must here be either to show that you know or to come to know. But knowledge is crucially different from mere true belief. All knowledge involves true belief; not all true belief constitutes knowledge. To have a true belief is simply and solely to believe that something is so, and to be in fact right. But someone may believe that this or that is so, and his belief may in fact be true, without its thereby and necessarily constituting knowledge. If a true belief is to achieve this more elevated status, then the believer has to be properly warranted so to believe. He must, that is, be in a position to know.

Obviously there is enormous scope for disagreement in particular cases: both about what is required in order to be in a position to know; and about whether these requirements have actually been satisfied. But the crucial distinction between believing truly and knowing is recognised as universally as the prior and equally vital distinction between believing and believing what is in fact true. If, for instance, there is a question whether a colleague performed some discreditable action, then all of us, though we have perhaps to admit that we cannot help believing that he did, are rightly scrupulous not to assert that this is known unless we have grounds sufficient to warrant the bolder claim. It is, therefore, not only incongruous but also scandalous in matters of life and death, and even of eternal life and death, to maintain that you know either on no ground at all, or on grounds of a kind which on other and comparatively minor issues you yourself would insist to be inadequate.

It is by reference to this inescapable demand for grounds that the presumption of atheism is justified. If it is to be established that there is a God, then we have to have good grounds for believing that this is indeed so. Until and unless some such grounds are produced we have literally no reason at all for believing; and in that situation the only reasonable posture must be that of either the negative atheist or the agnostic. So the onus of proof has to rest on the proposition. It must be up to them: first, to give whatever sense they choose to the word 'God', meeting any objection that so defined it would relate only to an incoherent pseudo-concept; and, second, to bring forward sufficient reasons to warrant their claim that, in their present sense of the word 'God', there is a God. The same applies, with appropriate alterations, if what is to be made out is, not that theism is known to be true, but only – more modestly – that it can be seen to be at least more or less probable.

4. *Objections to the presumption of atheism*

Once the nature of this presumption is understood, the supporting case is, as we have just seen in Section 3, short and simple.

(i) One reason why it may appear unacceptable is a confusion of contexts. In a theist or post-theist society it comes more easily to ask why a man is not a theist than why he is. Provided that the question is to be construed biographically this is no doubt methodologically inoffensive. But our concern here is not at all with biographical questions of why people came to hold whatever opinions they do hold. Rather it is with the need for opinions to be suitably grounded if they are to be rated as items of knowledge, or even of probable belief. The issue is: not what does or does not need to be explained biographically; but where the burden of theological proof should rest.

(ii) A more sophisticated objection of fundamentally the same sort would urge that our whole discussion has been too artificial and too general, and that any man's enquiries have to begin from wherever he happens to be: 'We cannot begin with complete doubt. We must begin with all the prejudices which we actually have. . . . These prejudices are not to be dispelled by a maxim' (Peirce, Volume V, pp. 156-157). Professor John Hick has urged, in *Theology Today* for 1967: 'The right question is whether it is rational for the religious man himself, given that his religious experience is coherent, persistent, and compelling, to affirm the reality of God. What is in question is not the rationality of an inference from certain psychological events to God as their cause; for the religious man no more infers the existence of God than we infer the existence of the visible world around us. What is in question is the rationality of the one who has the religious experiences. If we regard him as a rational person we must acknowledge that he is rational in believing what, given his experiences, he cannot help believing' (Hick, *loc. cit.*, pp. 86-87).

To the general point drawn from Peirce the answer comes from further reading of Peirce himself. He was, in the paper from which I quoted, arguing against the Cartesian programme of simultaneous, systematic, and (almost) universal doubt. Peirce did not want to suggest that it is impossible or wrong to subject any of our beliefs to critical scrutiny. In the same paragraph he continues: 'A person may, it is true, find reason to doubt what he began by believing; but in that case he doubts because he has a positive reason for it, and not on account of the Cartesian maxim.' One positive reason for being especially leery towards religious opinions is that these vary so very much from society to society; being, it seems, mainly determined, as Descartes has it, 'by custom and example'. The phrase occurs, in Part II of his *Discourse on the Method,* almost immediately after the observation: 'I took into account also the very different character which a person brought up from infancy in France or Germany exhibits, from that which . . . he would have possessed had he lived among the Chinese or with savages.'

To Hick it has at once to be conceded: that it is one thing to say that a belief is unfounded or well-founded; and quite another to say that it is irrational or rational for some particular person, in his particular time and circumstances, and with his particular experience and lack of experience, to hold or to reject that belief. Granted that his usually reliable Intelligence were sure that the enemy tank brigade was in the town, it was entirely reasonable for the General also to believe this. But the enemy tanks had in fact pulled back. Yet is was still unexceptionably sensible for the General on his part to refuse to expose his flank to those tanks which were in fact not there. This genuine and important distinction cannot, however, save the day for Hick.

In the first place, to show that someone may reasonably hold a particular belief, and even that he may properly claim that he knows it to be true, is at best still not to show that that belief is indeed well-grounded, much less that it constitutes an item of his knowledge.

Nor, second, is to accept the presumption of atheism as a methodological framework, as such: either to deprive anyone of his right 'to affirm the reality of God', or to require that to be respectable every conviction should first have been reached through the following of an ideally correct procedure. To insist on the correctness of this presumption as an initial presumption is to make a claim which is itself procedural rather than substantive; and the context for which this particular procedure is being recommended is that of justification rather than of discovery.

Once these fundamentals are appreciated, those for whom Hick is acting as spokesman should at first feel quite content. For on his account they consider that they have the very best of grounds for their beliefs. They regard their 'coherent, consistent, and compelling' religious experience as analogous to perception; and the man who can see something with his own eyes and feel it in his own hands is in a perfect position to know that it exists. His position is indeed so perfect that, as Hick says, it is wrong to speak here of evidence and inference. If he saw his wife in the act of intercourse with a lover then he no longer needs to infer her infidelity from bits and pieces of evidence. He has now what is better than inference; although for the rest of us, who missed this display, his testimony still constitutes an important part of the evidence in the case. The idiomatic expression, 'the evidence of my own eyes', derives its paradoxical piquancy from the fact that to see for oneself is better than to have evidence.

All this is true. Certainly, too, anyone who thinks that he can as it were see God must reject the suggestion that in so doing he infers 'from certain psychological events to God as their cause'. For to accept this account would be to call down upon his head all the insoluble difficulties which fall to the lot of all those who maintain that what we see, and all we ever really and directly see, is visual sense-data. And, furthermore, it is useful to be reminded that when we insist that knowledge as opposed to mere belief has to be adequately warranted, this grounding may be a matter either of having sufficient evidence or of being in a position to know directly and without evidence. So far, therefore, it might seem that Hick's objection was completely at cross-purposes; and that anyway his protégés have no need to appeal to the distinction between actual knowledge and what one may rationally and properly claim to know.

Wait a minute. The passage of Hick which has been under discussion was part of an attempt to show that criticism of the Argument from Religious Experience is irrelevant to such claims to as it were see God. But on the contrary: what such criticism usually challenges is just the vital assumption that having religious experience really is a kind of perceiving, and hence a sort of being in a position to know about its putative object. So this challenge provides just exactly that positive reason, which Peirce demanded, for doubting what, according to Hick, 'one who has the religious experiences . . . cannot help believing'. If, therefore, he persists in so believing, without even attempting to overcome this criticism, then it becomes impossible to vindicate his claims to be harbouring rational beliefs; much less items of authentic knowledge.

(iii) A third objection, of a different kind, starts from the assumption, mentioned already in Section 2 (i), that any programme to prove the existence of God is fundamentally misconceived; that this enterprise is on all fours with projects to square the circle or to construct a perpetual motion machine. The suggestion then is that the territory which reason cannot inhabit may nevertheless be freely colonised by faith: 'Faith alone can take you forward, when reason has gone as far as it can go'; and so on.

Ultimately perhaps it is impossible to establish the existence of God, or even to show that it is more or less probable. But, if so, this is not the correct moral: the rational man does not thereby become in this area free to believe, or not to believe, just as his fancy takes him. Faith, surely, should not be a leap in the dark but a leap towards the light. Arbitrarily to plump for some particular conviction, and then stubbornly to cleave to it, would be – to borrow the term which Thomas Aquinas employed in discussing faith, reason and revelation in the *Summa contra Gentiles* – 'frivolous' (I(vi): his Latin word is 'levis').[4] If your venture of faith is not to be arbitrary, irrational, and frivolous, you must have presentable reasons: first for making any such commitment in this area, an area in which by hypothesis the available grounds are insufficient to warrant any firm conclusion; and second for opting for one particular possibility rather than any of the other available alternatives. To most such offerings of reasons the presumption of atheism remains relevant. For though, again by the hypothesis, these cannot aspire to prove their conclusions they will usually embrace some estimation of their probability. If the onus of proof lies on the man who hopes definitively to establish the existence of God, it must also by the same token rest on the person who plans to make out only that this conclusion is more or less probable.

I put in the qualifications 'most' and 'usually' in order to allow for apologetic in the tradition of Pascal's Wager, which I shall discuss more fully in Chapter Five. Pascal makes no attempt in this most famous argument to show that his Roman Catholicism is true or probably true. The reasons which he suggests for making the recommended bet on his particular faith are reasons in the sense of motives rather than reasons in our previous sense of grounds. Conceding, if only for the sake of the present argument, that we can have no knowledge here, Pascal tries to justify as prudent a policy of systematic self-persuasion, rather than to provide grounds for thinking that the beliefs recommended are actually true.

5. *The Five Ways as an attempt to defeat the presumption of atheism*

I have tried, in the first four sections of this chapter, to explain what I mean by 'the presumption of atheism', to bring out by comparison with the presumption of innocence in law what such a presumption does and does not involve, to deploy a case for adopting my presumption of atheism, and to indicate the lines on which two sorts of objection may be met. Now, finally, I want to point out that Thomas Aquinas presented the Five Ways in his *Summa Theologica* as an attempt to defeat just such a presumption. My hope in this is, both to draw attention to something which seems generally to be overlooked, and by so doing to summon a massive authority in support of a thesis which many apparently find scandalous.

These most famous arguments were offered there originally, without any inhibition or equivocation, as proofs, period: 'I reply that we must say that God can be proved in five ways'; and the previous second Article, raising the question 'Whether the existence of God can be demonstrated?', gives the categorical affirmative answer that 'the existence of God . . . can be demonstrated' (I Q2 A3). It is worth stressing this point, since it is frequently denied. Thus, for instance, in an article in *Philosophy* for 1968, Dr L. C. Velecky asserts, without citation or compunction: 'He did not prove here the existence of God, nor, indeed, did he prove it anywhere else, for a good reason. According to Thomas, God's existence is unknowable and, hence, cannot be proved' (p. 226). The quotations just made from Aquinas ought to be decisive. Yet there seems to be quite a school of devout interpretation which waves aside what Aquinas straightforwardly said as almost irrelevant to the question of what he really meant.

Attention usually and understandably concentrates on the main body of the third Article, which is the part where Aquinas gives his five supposed proofs. But, as so often, it is rewarding to read the entire Article, and especially the second of the two Objections to which these are presented as a reply: 'Furthermore, what can be accounted for by fewer principles is not the product of more. But it seems that everything which can be observed in the world can be accounted for by other principles, on the assumption of the non-existence of God. Thus natural effects are explained by natural causes, while contrived effects are referred to human reason and will. So there is no need to postulate the existence of God.'

(i) The Five Ways are thus at least in one aspect an attempt to defeat this presumption of (an Aristotelian) atheist naturalism, by showing that the things 'which can be observed in the world' cannot 'be accounted for . . . on the assumption of the non-existence of God', and hence that there is 'need to postulate the existence of God'.

In this perspective it becomes easier to see why Aquinas makes so much use of Aristotelian scientific ideas in his arguments. That these are in fact much more dependent than is often realised on those now largely obsolete ideas is usefully emphasised in Anthony Kenny's *The Five Ways*. But Kenny does not bring out that they were deployed against a presumption of atheist naturalism.

Also one must never forget that Aquinas composed his own Objections, and hence that it was he who introduced into his formulation here the idea of (this Aristotelian) scientfic naturalism. No such idea is integral to the presumption of atheism as that has been construed in the present paper. When the addition is made the presumption can perhaps be labelled Stratonician. (Strato was the next but one in succession to Aristotle as head of the Lyceum, and was regarded by Bayle and Hume as the archetypal ancient spokesman for an atheist scientific naturalism).

By suggesting, a century before Ockham, an appeal to an Ockhamist principle of postulational economy Aquinas also indicates a reason for adopting such a presumption. The fact that Aquinas cannot be suspected of wanting to reach any sort of atheist conclusions can now be made to serve as a spectacular illustration of a point laboured in Section 2, that to adopt such a presumption is not to make an assumption. And the fact which has been put forward as an objection to this reading of Aquinas, that 'Thomas himself was never in the position of a Stratonician, nor did he live in a milieu in which Stratonicians were plentiful' (Velecky, *op. cit.*, pp. 225-226), is simply irrelevant. For the thesis that the onus of proof lies upon the theist is entirely independent of these historical and social facts. It is in the perspective provided by that thesis – a thesis apparently accepted by Aquinas himself – that we shall examine in Chapter Three and Chapter Five two famous attempts to defeat the presumption.

(ii) What is perhaps slightly awkward for present purposes is the formulation of the first Objection: 'It seems that God does not exist. For if of two contrary things one were to exist without limit the other would be totally eliminated. But what is meant by this word "God" is something good without limit. So if God were to have existed no evil would have been encountered. But evil is encountered in the world. Therefore, God does not exist.'

It would from my point of view have been better had this first Objection referred to possible difficulties and incoherencies in the meaning proposed for the word 'God'. Unfortunately it does not, although Aquinas is elsewhere acutely aware of such problems. The changes required, however, are, though important, not extensive. Certainly, the Objection as actually given is presented as one of the God hypothesis falsified by familiar fact. Yet a particular variety of the same general point could be represented as the detection of an incoherence, not in the proposed concept of God as such, but between that concept and another element in the theoretical structure in which it is normally involved.

The incoherence – or perhaps on this occasion I should say only the ostensible incoherence – is between the idea of creation, as necessarily involving complete, continual and absolute dependence of creature upon Creator, and the idea that creatures may nevertheless be sufficiently autonomous for their faults not to be also and indeed primarily His fault. The former idea, the idea of creation, is so essential that it provides the traditional criterion for distinguishing theism from deism. The latter is no less central to the three great theist systems of Judaism, Christianity, and Islam, since all three equally insist that creatures of the immaculate Creator are corrupted by sin. So where Aquinas put as his first Objection a statement of the traditional Problem of Evil, conceived as a problem of squaring the God hypothesis with certain undisputed facts, a redactor fully seized of the presumption of atheism as expounded in the present paper would refer instead to the ostensible incoherence, within the system itself, between the concept of creation by a flawless Creator and the notion of His creatures flawed by their sins. As for whether this incoherence is not only ostensible but also actual I shall have something to say in Chapter Seven.

NOTES

1. This and some later translations from the Latin are mine.
2. See Chapter VI of Lewis Carroll's *Through the Looking Glass:*

> 'But "glory" doesn't mean "a nice knock-down argument" ', Alice objected.
> 'When I use a word', Humpty Dumpty said in rather a scornful tone, 'it means just what I choose it to mean—neither more nor less.'
> 'The question is', said Alice, 'whether you *can* make words mean so many different things.'
> 'The question is', said Humpty Dumpty, 'which is to be master—that's all.'

3. See the paper 'Presumptions' by my former colleague Patrick Day in the *Proceedings of the XIVth International Congress of Philosophy* (Vienna, 1968), Vol V, at p. 140. I am pleased that it was I who first suggested to him an exploration of this unfrequented philosophical territory.
4. The whole passage, in which Aquinas gives his reasons for believing that the Christian candidate does, and that of Muhammad does not, constitute an authentic revelation of God should be compared with some defence of the now widely popular assumption that the contents of a religious faith must be without evidential warrant.

   A. C. MacIntyre, for instance, while he was still himself a Christian, argued with great vigour for the Barthian thesis that "Belief cannot argue with unbelief: it can only preach to it". Thus he urged: ". . . suppose religion could be provided with a method of proof . . . since the Christian faith sees true religion only in a free decision made in faith and love, the religion would by this vindication be destroyed. For all possibility of free choice would have been done away. Any objective justification of belief would have the same effect . . . faith too would have been eliminated" (MacIntyre, p. 209).

   Now, first, in so far as this account is correct any commitment to a system of religious belief has to be made altogether without evidencing reasons. MacIntyre himself concludes with a quotation from John Donne to illustrate the "confessional voice" of faith, commenting: "The man who speaks like this is beyond argument" (MacIntyre, p. 211). But this, we must insist, would be nothing to be proud of. It is certainly no compliment, even if it were a faithful representation, to portray the true believer as necessarily irrational and a bigot.

Furthermore, second, it is not the case that where sufficient evidence is available there can be no room for choice. Men can, and constantly do, choose to deceive themselves about the most well-evidenced, inconvenient truths. Also no recognition of any facts, however clear, is by itself sufficient to guarantee one allegiance and to preclude its opposite. MacIntyre needs to extend his reading of the Christian poets to the greatest of them all. For the hero of Milton's *Paradise Lost* had the most enviably full and direct knowledge of God. Yet Lucifer, if any creature could, chose freely to rebel.

Flew also refers to

Peirce, C. S. *Collected Papers*. Harvard University Press, from 1934.

Hick, J. H. (ed.) *Classical and Contemporary Readings in the Philosophy of Religion*. Englewood Cliffs, N. J., Prentice-Hall, 1970.

MacIntyre, A. C. (ed.) *Metaphysical Beliefs*. London, S.C.M., 1957.

QUESTIONS for further discussion:

An alleged parallel is examined between, on the one hand our knowledge of the physical world by sense-perception and, on the other, knowledge of God by way of religious experience. Hick has suggested that just as sense-experience which is coherent, consistent and compelling is our (non-evidential) ground for our rational belief in the existence of the physical world, so religious experience can afford the ground for belief in the existence of God. Flew's counter is that it is always possible to doubt whether religious experience *is* cognitive awareness of some reality which exists independently of our experience, and that unless Hick can rationally overcome this doubt, his proposal is valueless. Is the doubt of which Flew speaks here the doubt that may attach to a particular experience as to whether on that particular occasion hallucination or misinterpretation has been present, so that what is supposed to be seen (or touched) is not in fact present at all? Or is Flew raising, rather, the doubt over whether all the experience we have provides ground for belief in any real world, physical or religious, whatever, existing independently of our minds?

If his question is the latter he may give as his answer that the character of experience supposedly of the physical world is not such as to justify belief in that world. In that case, he will hold it unreasonable to believe in the physical world, which *may* invite a response that Flew's standards of reasonableness are not acceptable. If, however, as seems likelier, Flew considers that our sense-experience is such ('coherent, consistent and compelling' in the relevant respects, perhaps) as to justify belief in a physical world, but not in a religious, or spiritual, world. In that case a response might be that it is open to investigation how far religious experience is or can be coherent, consistent and compelling. And if it is in this way even a possibility that religious experience provides grounds for belief in a world of religious reality, including, it may be, God, then the concept of 'god' has a use.

If the former question is the one which concerns Flew, then he must suppose that there are ways of distinguishing particular trustworthy genuinely perceptual experiences from hallucinatory or otherwise untrustworthy ones. Some writers have spoken of these latter as 'wild', not cohering with, not being consistent with the rest of our experience, in the way that trustworthy experiences would. However the distinction is made, it will be a matter for investigation once more whether a particular experience in question has the marks of a 'wild', or cohering, experience. (Related issues arise in later papers in this volume, on the topic of religious experience.)

One last line of questioning suggests itself as a result of exploring the preceding issues: perhaps Flew's concern is that, as yet, no adequate account has been sketched as to what features of some religious experience, actual or possible, will justify the supposition that it is experience *of* a reality existing independently of our experience. We have some idea of how to distinguish experiences which are genuine perceptions of the physical world, from those which are not. Perhaps Flew's worry is that, if we lack the parallel ability in respect of the 'spiritual' world the offering of parallels between religious experience and sense-perception will be, at best, premature. If this question is to be pursued, one obvious way would appear to be to listen to the mystics, to see whether, and if so, how, they distinguish the genuine religious experience from the misleading, and maybe, how far they share the 'spiritual' world so as to be able to talk about it.

Paper III
Introductory Groundwork

The argument which is set out in steps 1–5 near the beginning of the following paper is one of several arguments known as cosmological arguments. Four of the 'Five Ways' of Thomas Aquinas are cosmological arguments. Leibniz and Samuel Clarke proposed distinguishable influential versions. As Professor Rowe's essay, with its footnotes, makes clear, the 'two criticisms' with which he deals are criticisms put by Hume in the eighteenth century and Russell in the twentieth; in both cases the critical points are put rather briefly, and with such an influence as few philosophers can have exercised by two or three sentences.[1] There are other difficulties to be faced by anyone proposing any cosmological arguments, but in modern debate these two have loomed largest, and have very widely been thought to prevail. Accordingly although Rowe's discussion might seem to be rather restricted, in discussing these points alone, many modern philosophers would be disinclined to engage in any further work on this argument, unless these points are called in question. Those who wish to consult Professor Rowe's fuller discussion of contentious issues raised by the argument should consult his book *The Cosmological Argument*, Princeton, 1975.[2]

NOTES

1. Hume's are in section IX of the *Dialogues Concerning Natural Religion*, and Russell's in his debate with Father Copleston, later printed in *Why I am not a Christian*, London, 1957, ch. 13.
2. Rowe devotes most attention to Samuel Clarke's version of the argument; for a discussion given more to Leibniz, see Swinburne's *The Existence of God*, ch. 7.

Two Criticisms of the Cosmological Argument

W. L. ROWE

In this paper I wish to consider two major criticisms that have been advanced against the Cosmological Argument for the existence of God, criticisms which many philosophers regard as constituting a decisive refutation of that argument. Before stating and examining these objections it will be helpful to have before us a version of the Cosmological Argument. The Cosmological Argument has two distinct parts. The first part is an argument to establish the existence of a necessary being. The second part is an argument to establish that this necessary being is God. The two objections I shall consider are directed against the first part of the Cosmological Argument. Using the expression 'dependent being' to mean 'a being that has the reason for its existence in the causal efficacy or nature of some other being', and the expression 'independent being' to mean 'a being that has the reason for its existence within its own nature', we may state the argument for the existence of a necessary being as follows:

1. Every being is either a dependent being or an independent being; therefore,
2. Either there exists an independent being or every being is dependent;
3. It is false that every being is dependent; therefore,
4. There exists an independent being; therefore,
5. There exists a necessary being.

This argument consists of two premises – propositions (1) and (3) – and three inferences. The first inference is from (1) to (2), the second from (2) and (3) to (4), and the third inference is from (4) to (5). Of the premises neither is obviously true, and of the inferences only the first and second are above suspicion. Before discussing the main subject of this paper – the reasoning in support of proposition (3) and the two major objections that have been advanced against that reasoning – I want to say something about the other questionable parts of the argument; namely proposition (1) and the inference from (1) to (5).

Proposition (1) expresses what we may call the strong form of the Principle of Sufficient Reason. It insists not only that those beings which begin to exist must have a cause or explanation (the weak form of the Principle of Sufficient Reason) but that absolutely every being must have an explanation of its existing rather than not existing – the explanation lying either within the causal efficacy of some other being or within the thing's own nature. In an earlier paper I examined this Principle in some detail.[1] The objections I wish to consider in this paper are, I believe, independent of the Principle of Sufficient Reason. That is, these objections are meant to refute the argument even if the first premise is true. This being so it will facilitate our examination of these two objections if we take proposition (1) as an unquestioned premise throughout our discussion. Accordingly, in this paper proposition (1) will function as an axiom in our reasoning. This, of course, should not be taken as implying that I think the first premise of the argument is true.

The inference from proposition (4) to proposition (5) is not considered in this paper. Indeed, for purposes of this paper we could have ended the statement of the argument with proposition (4). I have included the inference from (4) to (5) simply because it is an important element in the first part of the Cosmological Argument. Proposition (4) asserts the existence of a being that has the reason or explanation of its existence within its own nature. Proposition (5) asserts the existence of a necessary being. By 'a necessary being' is meant a being whose nonexistence is a logical impossibility.[2] Many philosophers have argued that it is logically impossible for there to be a necessary being in this sense of 'necessary being'. Hence, even if the two objections I shall examine in this paper can be met, the defender of the Cosmological Argument must still face objections not only to the inference from (4) to (5) but to (5) itself. But again, this is a matter that I shall not pursue in this paper. Unlike proposition (1), however, which I treat as an unquestioned assumption, neither proposition (5) nor the inference from (4) to (5) will be appealed to in this paper. In what follows we may simply ignore that part of the argument. Indeed, our attention will be focused entirely on proposition (3), the reasoning that supports it, and the two major criticisms that have been advanced against that reasoning.

Proposition (3) asserts that it is false that every being is dependent. For what reasons? Well, if every being that exists (or ever existed) is dependent then the whole of existing things, it would seem, consists of a collection of dependent beings, that is, a collection of beings each member of which exists by reason of the causal efficacy of some other being. This collection would have to contain an infinite number of members. For suppose it contained a finite number, let us say three, *a, b,* and *c.* Now if in Scotus's phrase 'a circle of causes is inadmissible' then if *c* is caused by *b* and *b* by *a, a* would exist without a cause, there being no other member of the collection that could be its cause. But in that case *a* would not be what by supposition it is, namely a *dependent* being. Hence, if we grant that a circle of causes is inadmissible it is impossible that the whole of existing things should consist of a collection of dependent beings *finite* in number.

Suppose, then, that the dependent beings making up the collection are infinite in number. Why is it impossible that the whole of existing things should consist of such a collection? The proponent of the Cosmological Argument answers as follows.[3] The infinite collection *itself,* he argues, requires an explanation of its existence. For since it is true of each member of the collection that it might not have existed, it is true of the whole infinite collection that it might not have existed. But if the entire infinite collection might not have existed there must be some explanation of why it exists rather than not. The explanation cannot lie in the causal efficacy of some being outside of the collection since by supposition the collection includes every being that is or ever was. Nor can the explanation of why there is an infinite collection be found within the collection itself, for since no member of the collection is independent, has the reason of its existence within itself, the collection as a whole cannot have the reason of its existence within itself. Thus the conception of an infinite collection of dependent beings is the conception of something whose existence has no explanation whatever. But since premise (1) tells us that whatever exists has an explanation for its existence, either within itself or in the causal efficacy of some other being, it cannot be that the whole of existing things consists of an infinite collection of dependent beings.

The reasoning developed here is exhibited as follows:

1. If every being is dependent then the whole of existing things consists of an infinite collection of dependent beings;

2. If the whole of existing things consists of an infinite collection of dependent beings then the infinite collection itself must have an explanation of its existence;

3. If the existence of the infinite collection of dependent beings has an explanation then the explanation must lie either in the causal efficacy of some being outside the collection or it must lie within the infinite collection itself;

4. The explanation of the existence of the infinite collection of dependent beings cannot lie in the causal efficacy of some being outside the collection;

5. The explanation of the existence of the infinite collection of dependent beings cannot lie within the collection itself; therefore,

6. There is no explanation of the infinite collection of dependent beings; (from 3, 4, and 5), therefore,

7. It is false that the whole of existing things consists of an infinite collection of dependent beings; (from 2 and 6), therefore,

8. It is false that every being is dependent. (from 1 and 7).

Perhaps every premise in this argument is open to criticism. I propose here, however, to consider what I regard as the two major criticisms that have been advanced against this reasoning in support of proposition (3) of the main argument. The first of these criticisms may be construed as directed against premise (2) of the above argument. According to this criticism it *makes no sense* to apply the notion of cause or explanation to the totality of things, and the arguments used to show that the whole of existing things must have a cause or explanation are *fallacious*. Thus in his B.B.C. debate with Father Copleston, Bertrand Russell took the view that the concept of cause is inapplicable to the universe conceived of as the total collection of things. When pressed by Copleston as to how he could rule out 'the legitimacy of asking the question how the total, or anything at all comes to be there,' Russell responded: 'I can illustrate what seems to me your fallacy. Every man who exists has a mother, and it seems to me your argument is that therefore the human race must have a mother, but obviously the human race hasn't a mother – that's a different logical sphere.'[4]

The second major criticism is directed at premise (5). According to this criticism it is *intelligible* to ask for an explanation of the existence of the infinite collection of dependent beings. But the answer to this question, so the criticism goes, is provided once we learn that each member of the infinite collection has an explanation of its existence. Thus Hume remarks: 'Did I show you the particular causes of each individual in a collection of twenty particles of matter, I should think it very unreasonable, should you afterwards ask me, what was the cause of the whole twenty. This is sufficiently explained in explaining the cause of the parts.'[5]

These two criticisms express the major reasons philosophers have given for rejecting what undoubtedly is the most important part of the Cosmological Argument; namely, that portion of the argument which seeks to establish that not every being can be a dependent being. In this paper my aim is to defend the Cosmological Argument against both of these criticisms. I shall endeavour to show that both these criticisms rests on a philosophical mistake.

The first criticism draws attention to what appears to be a fatal flaw in the Cosmological Argument. It seems that the proponent of the argument (i) ascribes to the infinite collection itself a property (having a cause or explanation) which is applicable only to the members of that collection, and (ii) does so by means of a fallacious inference from a proposition about the members of the collection to a proposition about the collection itself. There are, then, two alleged mistakes committed here. The first error is, perhaps, a category mistake – the ascription to the collection of a property applicable only to the members of the collection. As Russell would say, the collection, in comparison with its members, belongs to a 'different logical sphere.' The second error is apparently what leads the proponent of the Cosmological Argument to make the first error. He ascribes the property of having an explanation to the infinite collection because he *infers* that the infinite collection must have a cause or explanation from the premise that each of its members has a cause. But to infer this, Russell suggests, is as fallacious as to infer that the human race must have a mother because each member of the human race has a mother.

That the proponent of the Cosmological Argument ascribes the property of having a cause or explanation to the infinite collection of dependent beings is certainly true. That to do so is a category mistake is, I think, questionable. But before pursuing this point I want to deal with the second charge. The main question we must consider in connection with the second charge is whether the Cosmological Argument involves the inference: Every member of the infinite collection has an explanation of its existence; therefore, the infinite collection itself has an explanation of its existence. As we have seen, Russell thinks Copleston has employed this inference in coming to the conclusion that there must be an explanation for the totality of things, and not simply for each of the things making up that totality.

Perhaps some proponents of the Cosmological Argument have used the argument that Russell regards as fallacious. But not all of them have.[6] Moreover, there is no need to employ such an inference since in its first premise the Cosmological Argument has available a principle from which it follows that the infinite collection of dependent beings must have an explanation of its existence. Thus one famous exponent of the argument – Samuel Clarke – reasons that the infinite collection of beings must have an explanation of its existence by appealing to the strong form of the Principle of Sufficient Reason. The principle assures us that whatever exists has an explanation of its existence. But if there exists an infinite succession or collection of dependent beings then that collection or succession, Clarke reasons, must have an explanation of its existence. Hence, we can, I think, safely dismiss the charge that the Cosmological Argument involves an erroneous inference from the premise that the members of a collection have a certain property to the conclusion that the collection itself must have that property.

We must now deal with the question whether it makes *sense* to ascribe the property of having an explanation or cause to the infinite collection of dependent beings. Clearly only if it does make sense is the reasoning in support of proposition (3) of the main argument acceptable. Our question, then, is whether it makes sense to ask for a cause or explanation of the entire universe, conceiving the universe as an infinite collection of dependent beings.

One recent critic of the Cosmological Argument, Ronald Hepburn, has stated our problem as follows:

> When we are seriously speaking of absolutely everything
> there is, are we speaking of something that requires a cause, in
> the way that events *in* the universe may require causes? What
> indeed can be safely said at all about the totality of things? For a
> great many remarks that one can make with perfect propriety
> about limited things quite obviously can*not* be made about the
> cosmos itself. It cannot, for instance, be said meaningfully to be

'above' or 'below' anything, although things-in-the-universe can be so related to one another. Whatever we might claim to be '*below* the universe' would turn out to be just some more *universe*. We should have been relating part to part, instead of relating the whole to something not-the-universe. The same applies to 'outside the universe'. We can readily imagine a boundary, a garden wall, shall we say, round something that we want to call the universe. But if we imagine ourselves boring a hole through that wall and pushing a stick out *beyond* it into a nameless zone 'outside', we should still not in fact have given meaning to the phrase 'outside the universe'. For the place into which the stick was intruding would deserve to be called a part of the universe (even if consisting of empty space, no matter) just as much as the area within the walls. We should have demonstrated *not* that the universe has an outside, but that what we took to be the whole universe was not really the whole.

Our problem is this. Supposing we could draw up a list of questions that can be asked about objects in the universe, but cannot be asked about the *whole* universe: would the question, 'Has it a cause?' be on that list? One thing is clear. Whether or not this question is on the proscribed list, we are not entitled to argue as the Cosmological Argument does that *because* things in the world have causes, therefore the sum of things must also have *its* cause. No more (as we have just seen) can we argue from the fact that things in the world have tops and bottoms, insides and outsides, and are related to other things, to the belief that the universe has its top and bottom, inside and outside, and is related to a supra-cosmical something.[7]

In this passage Hepburn (i) points out that some properties (e.g., 'above', 'below', etc.) of things in the universe cannot properly be ascribed to the total universe, (ii) raises the question whether 'having a cause' is such a property, and (iii) concludes that '. . . we are not entitled to argue as the Cosmological Argument does that *because* things in the world have causes, therefore, the sum of things must also have *its* cause. We noted earlier that the Cosmological Argument (i.e., the version we are examining) does not argue that the sum of things (the infinite collection of dependent beings) must have a cause *because* each being in the collection has a cause. Thus we may safely ignore Hepburn's main objection. However, his other two points are well taken. There certainly are properties which it makes sense to apply to things within a collection but which it makes no sense to apply to the collection itself. What assurance do we have that 'having a cause' is not such a property?

Suppose we are holding in our hands a collection of ten marbles. Not only would each marble have a definite weight but the collection itself would have a weight. Indeed, from the premise that each marble weighs more than an ounce we could infer validly that the collection itself weighs more than an ounce. This example shows that it is not always fallacious to infer that a collection has a certain property from the premise that each member of the collection has that property.[8] But the collection in this example is, we might say, *concrete* rather than *abstract*. That is, we are here considering the collection as itself a physical entity, an aggregate of marbles. This, of course, is not a collection in the sense of a class or set of things. Holding several marbles in my hands I can consider the *set* whose members are those marbles. The set itself, being an *abstract* entity, rather than a physical heap, has no weight. Just as the set of human beings has no mother, so the set whose members are marbles in my hand has no weight. Therefore, in considering whether it makes sense to speak of the infinite collection of dependent beings as having a cause or explanation of its existence it is important to decide whether we are speaking of a collection as a *concrete* entity – for example, a physical whole or aggregate – or an *abstract* entity.

Suppose we view the infinite collection of dependent beings as itself a concrete entity. So far as the Cosmological Argument is concerned one advantage of so viewing it is that it is understandable why it might have the property of having a cause or explanation of its existence. For concrete entities – physical objects, events, physical heaps – can be caused. Thus if the infinite collection is a concrete entity it may well make sense to ascribe to it the property of having a cause or explanation.

But such a view of the infinite collection is implausible, if not plainly incorrect. Many collections of physical things cannot possibly be themselves concrete entities. Think, for example, of the collection whose members are the largest prehistoric beast, Socrates, and the Empire State Building. By any stretch of the imagination can we view this collection as itself a concrete thing? Clearly we cannot. Such a collection must be construed as an *abstract* entity, a class or set.[9] But if

39

there are many collections of beings which cannot be concrete entities, what grounds have we for thinking that on the supposition that every being that is or ever was is dependent the collection of those beings would itself be a concrete thing such as a physical heap? At any rate our knowledge of the things (both past and present) comprising the universe and their interrelations would have to be much greater than it presently is before we would be entitled to view the *sum* of concrete things, past and present, as itself something *concrete*.

But if the infinite collection of dependent beings is to be understood as an abstract entity, say the set whose members include all the beings that are or ever were, haven't we conceded the point to Russell? A set or class conceived of as an abstract entity has no weight, isn't below or above anything, and can't be thought of as being caused or brought into being. Thus if the infinite collection is a set, an abstract entity, isn't Russell right in charging that it makes no more sense to ascribe the property of having a cause or an explanation to the infinite collection than it does to ascribe the property of having a mother to the human race?

Suppose that every being that is or ever was is dependent. Suppose further that the number of such beings is infinite. Let A be the set consisting of these beings. Thus no being exists or ever existed that is not a member of A. Does it make *sense* to ask for an explanation of A's existence? We do, of course, ask questions about sets which are equivalent to questions about their members. For example, 'Is set X included in set Y?' is equivalent to the question 'Is every member of X a member of Y?' I suggest that the question 'Why does A exist?' be taken to mean 'Why does A have the members that it does rather than some other members or none at all?' Consider, for example, the set of men. Let M be this set. The question 'Why does M exist?' is perhaps odd if we understand it as a request for an explanation of the existence of an abstract entity. But the question 'Why does M exist?' may be taken to mean 'Why does M have the members it has rather than some other members or none at all?' So understood the form of words 'Why does M exist?' does, I think, ask an intelligible question. It is a contingent fact that Hitler existed. Indeed, it is a contingent fact that any men exist at all. One of Leibniz' logically possible worlds is a world that included some members of M, for example Socrates and Plato, but not others, say Hitler and Stalin. Another is a world in which the set of men is entirely empty and therefore identical with the null set.

Why is it then, that M exists? That is, why does M have just the members it has rather than some other members or none at all? Not only is this question intelligible but we seem to have some idea of what its answer is. Presumably, the theory of evolution might be a part of the explanation of why M is not equivalent to the null set and why its members have certain properties rather than others.

But if the question 'Why does M exist?' makes sense, why should not the question 'Why does A exist?' also make sense? A is the set of dependent beings. In asking why A exists we are not asking for an explanation of the existence of an abstract entity, we are asking why A has the members it has rather than some other members or none at all. I submit that this question does make sense. Moreover, I think it is precisely this question that the proponents of the Cosmological Argument were asking when they asked for an explanation of the existence of the infinite collection or succession of dependent beings.[10] Of course, it is one thing for a question to make sense and another thing for there to be an answer to it.

The interpretation I have given to the question 'Why does A exist?' is somewhat complex. For according to this interpretation what is being asked is not simply why does A have members rather than having none, but also why does A have just the members it does rather than having some other members. Although the proponents of the Cosmological Argument do seem to interpret the question in this way, it will facilitate our discussion if we simplify the interpretation somewhat by focusing our attention solely on the question why A has the members it has rather than having none. Hence, for purposes of simplification, in what follows I shall take the question 'Why does A exist?' to mean 'Why does A have the members it has rather than not having any?'

For any being to be a member of A it is necessary and sufficient that it have the reason of its existence in the causal efficacy of some other being. Imagine the following state of affairs. A has exactly three members: a_1, a_2, and a_3. a_3 exists by reason of the causal efficacy of a_2 and a_2 exists by reason of the causal efficacy of a_1. There exists an *eternal* being b that does not exist by reason of the causal efficacy of any other being. Since b is not a dependent being, b is not a member of A. At a certain time a_1 came into existence by reason of the causal efficacy of b. Clearly the question 'Why does A exist?' when taken to mean 'Why does A have the members it has rather than none at all?', makes sense when asked within the context of this imagined state of affairs. Indeed, part of the answer to the question would involve reference to *b* and its causal efficacy in bringing about the existence of one of the members of A, namely a_1.

What this case shows is that the question 'Why does A exist?' is not always (i.e., in every context) meaningless. If Russell holds that the question is meaningless in the framework of the Cosmological Argument it must be because of some special assumption about A that forms part of the context of the Cosmological Argument. The assumption in question undoubtedly is that absolutely every being is dependent. On this assumption every being that is or ever was has membership in A and A has an infinite number of members.

Perhaps Russell's view is that within the context of the assumption that *every* being is dependent it makes no sense to ask why A has the members it has rather than none at all. It makes no sense, he might argue, for two reasons. First, on the assumption that every being is dependent there could not be such a thing as the *set* A whose members are all dependent beings. For the set A is, although abstract, presumably a being. But if every being is dependent then A would have to be dependent and therefore a member of itself. But apart from whatever difficulties arise when a set is said to be a member of itself, it would seem to make little sense to think of an abstract entity, such as a set, as being caused, as having the reason of its existence within the causal efficacy of some other being.

Second, Russell might argue that the assumption that every being is dependent and therefore a member of A rules out the possibility of any answer to the question why A has the members it has rather than none at all. For on that assumption our question about A is in effect a question about the totality of things. And, as Russell observes, 'I see no reason whatsoever to suppose that the total has any cause whatsoever.'[11]

Neither of these reasons suffices to show that our question about A is meaningless. The first reason does, however, point up the necessity of introducing some restriction on the assumption 'Every being is dependent' in order that abstract entities like numbers and sets not fall within the scope of the expression 'Every being'. Such a restriction will obviate the difficulty that A is said to be both a member of itself and dependent. I propose the following rough restriction. In speaking of beings we shall restrict ourselves to beings that *could be caused* to exist by some other being or *could be causes* of the existence of other beings. God (if he exists), a man, the sun, a stone are beings of this sort. Presumably, numbers, sets and the like are not. The assumption that every being is dependent is to be understood under this restriction. That is, we are here assuming that every being of the sort described by the restriction is *in fact* a being that exists by reason of the causal efficacy of some other being. The second reason given confuses the issue of whether a question makes sense, is meaningful, with the issue of whether a question has an answer. Of course, given the assumption that every being is a member of A we cannot expect to find the cause or reason of A's existence in some being that is not a member of A. If the explanation for A's existence cannot be found within A itself then we must conclude that there can be no explanation for the infinite collection of dependent beings. But this is to say only that on our assumption that every being is dependent there is no answer to the question 'Why does A exist?' It is one thing for a question not to have an answer and quite another thing for the question to be *meaningless*.

We have been examining the first of the two major criticisms philosophers have directed at the reasoning the Cosmological Argument provides in support of the proposition that not every being is dependent. The heart of this criticism is that it *makes no sense* to ascribe the property of having a cause or explanation to the infinite collection of dependent beings. This criticism, I think, has been shown to be correct in one way, but incorrect in another. If we construe the infinite collection of dependent beings as an abstract entity, a set, it perhaps does not make sense to claim that something caused the existence of this abstract entity. But the question 'Why does A exist?' may be interpreted to mean 'Why does A have the members it does rather than none at all?' I have argued that taken in this way the question 'Why does A exist?' is a *meaningful* question.

According to the Principle of Sufficient Reason there must be an answer to the question 'Why does A exist?', an explanation of the existence of the infinite collection of dependent beings. Moreover, the explanation must lie either in the causal efficacy of some being outside of the collection or it must lie within the collection itself. But since by supposition every being is dependent – and therefore in the collection – there is no being outside the collection whose causal efficacy might explain the existence of the collection. Therefore, either the collection has the explanation of its existence within itself *or* there can be no explanation of its existence. If the first alternative is rejected then since the Principle of Sufficient Reason requires that everything has an explanation of its existence we must reject the supposition that every being is dependent. For on that supposition there is no explanation for why there is an infinite collection of dependent beings.

The second major criticism argues that the proponent of the Cosmological Argument is mistaken in thinking that the explanation of the existence of the infinite collection cannot be found within the collection itself. The explanation of the existence of the collection is provided, so the criticism goes, once we learn what the explanation is of each of the members of the collection. As we noted earlier, this criticism was succinctly expressed by Hume in his remark: 'Did I show you the particular causes of each individual in a collection of twenty particles of matter, I should think it very unreasonable, should you afterwards ask me, what was the cause of the whole twenty. This is sufficiently explained in explaining the cause of the parts.' Applying this objection to the infinite collection of dependent beings, we obtain the result that to explain the existence of the infinite collection, A, amounts to no more than explaining the existence of each of its members. Now, of course, A is unlike Hume's collection of twenty particles in that we cannot give *individual* explanations for each of the members of A. For since A has an infinite number of members we would have to give an infinite number of explanations. But our inability to give a particular explanation for each of the members of A does not imply that there is any member of A for whose existence there is no explanation. Indeed, from the fact that each member of A is dependent (i.e., has the reason of its existence in the causal efficacy of some other being) we know that every member of A has an explanation of its existence, and from the assumption that every being is a member of A we know that for each member of A the explanation lies in the causal efficacy of some other member of A. But, so the criticism goes, if every member of A has an explanation of its existence then the existence of A has been sufficiently explained. For to explain why a certain collection of things exists it is sufficient to explain the existence of each of its members. Hence, since we know that the existence of every one of A's members is explained we know that the existence of the collection A is explained.

This forceful criticism, originally advanced by Hume, has gained wide acceptance in contemporary philosophy. Indeed, the only remaining problem seems to be to explain why the proponents of the Cosmological Argument failed to see that to explain the existence of all the members of a collection is to explain the existence of the collection. In restating Hume's criticism, Paul Edwards suggests that perhaps they may have been misled by grammar.

> The demand to find the cause of the series as a whole rests on the erroneous assumption that the series is something over and above the members of which it is composed. It is tempting to suppose this, at least by implication, because the word 'series' is a noun like 'dog' or 'man'. Like the expression 'this dog' or 'this man' the phrase 'this series' is easily taken to designate an individual object. But reflection shows this to be an error. If we have explained the individual members there is nothing additional left to be explained. Suppose I see a group of five Eskimos standing on the corner of Sixth Avenue and 50th Street and I wish to explain why the group came to New York. Investigation reveals the following stories:
> Eskimo No. 1 did not enjoy the extreme cold in the polar region and decided to move to a warmer climate.
> No. 2 is the husband of Eskimo No. 1. He loves her dearly and did not wish to live without her.
> No. 3 is the son of Eskimos 1 and 2. He is too small and too weak to oppose his parents.
> No. 4 saw an advertisement in the *New York Times* for an Eskimo to appear on television.
> No. 5 is a private detective engaged by the Pinkerton Agency to keep an eye on Eskimo No. 4.
> Let us assume that we have explained in the case of each of the five Eskimos why he or she is in New York. Somebody then asks: 'All right, but what about the group as a whole; why is *it* in New York?' This would plainly be an absurd question. There is no group over and above the five members, and if we have explained why each of the five members is in New York we have *ipso facto* explained why the group is there. It is just as absurd to ask for the cause of the series as a whole as distinct from asking for the causes of the individual members.[12]

The principle underlying the Hume-Edwards criticism may be stated as follows: *If the existence of every member of a set is explained the*

45

existence of that set is thereby explained. This principle seems to be a corollary of our interpretation of the question 'Why does this set exist?' For on our interpretation once it is explained why the set has the members it has rather than none at all it is thereby explained why the set exists. And it would seem that if a set A has, say, three members, a_1, a_2, and a_3, then if we explain the existence of a_1, a_2, and a_3 we have explained why A has the members it has rather than none at all. Thus the principle that underlies the second major criticism seems to be implied by our conception of what is involved in explaining the existence of a set.

The principle underlying the Hume-Edwards criticism seems plausible enough when restricted to finite sets, i.e., sets with a finite number of members. But the principle is false, I believe, when extended to infinite sets in which the explanation of each member's existence is found in the causal efficacy of some other member. Consider M, the set of men. Suppose M consists of an infinite number of members, each member owing its existence to some other member which generated it. Suppose further that to explain the existence of a given man it is sufficient to note that he was begotten by some other man. That is, where x and y are men and x begat y we allow that the existence of y is explained by the causal efficacy of x. On these suppositions it is clear that the antecedent of the principle is satisfied with respect to M. For every member of M has an explanation of its existence. But does it follow that the existence of M has an explanation? I think not. We do not have an explanation of the existence of M until we have an explanation of why M has the members it has rather than none at all. But clearly if *all* we know is that there always have been men and that every man's existence is explained by the causal efficacy of some other man, we do not know *why* there always have been men rather than none at all. If I ask why M has the members it does rather than none, it is no answer to say that M always had members. We may, I suppose, answer the question 'Why does M have the *presently existing* members it has?' by saying that M always had members and there were men who generated the presently existing men. But in asking why M has the members it does rather than none at all we are not asking why M has the presently existing members it has. To make this clear, we may rephrase our question as follows: 'Why is it that M has now and always had members rather than never having had any members at all?' Surely we have not

46

learned the answer to this question when we have learned that there always have been members of M and that each member's existence is explained by the causal efficacy of some other member.

What we have just seen is that from the fact that the existence of each member of a collection is explained it does not follow that the existence of the collection is thereby explained. It does not follow because when the collection (set) has an infinite number of members, each member's existence having its explanation in the causal efficacy of *some other member,* it is true that the existence of every member has an explanation and yet still an open question whether the existence of the set has an explanation. To explain the existence of a set we must explain why it has the members it has rather than none. But clearly if every member's existence is explained by some other *member* then although the existence of every member has an explanation it is still unexplained why the set has the members it has, rather than none at all.

Put somewhat differently, we have seen that the fact (assuming for the moment that it is a fact) that there always have been men, each man's existence brought about by some other man, is insufficient to explain *why* it is a fact that there always have been men rather than a fact that there never have been any men. If someone asks us to explain why there always have been men rather than never having been any it would not suffice for us to observe that there always have been men and each man has been brought into existence by some other man.

I have argued that the second major criticism rests on a false principle, namely, that if the existence of every member of a set is explained then the existence of that set is thereby explained. This principle, so far as I can determine, is true when restricted to sets with a *finite* number of members. For example, if a set A has two members, a_1 and a_2, and if we explain a_2 by a_1 and a_1 by some being b that caused a_1 then, I think, we have explained the existence of A. In any case we have explained why A has members rather than none at all. Thus I am not claiming that the principle underlying Hume's objection is always false. Indeed, as I've just indicated, it is easy to provide an example of a finite set of which the principle is true. And perhaps it is just this feature of the principle – i.e., its plausibility when applied to finite sets such as Hume's collection of twenty particles and Edwards' five Eskimos – that has led Hume and many philosophers since Hume to reject the Cosmological Argument's thesis that even if every member of the infinite succession of dependent beings has an explanation the infinite succession itself is not thereby explained. If so, then the mistake Hume and his successors have made is to assume that a principle which is true of all finite sets also is true of all infinite sets.

We know, for example, that if we have a set B consisting of five members and a set C consisting of three of the members of B, the members of C cannot be put in one-to-one correspondence with those of B. In reflecting on this fact, it is tempting to conclude that for *any* two sets X and Y, if all the members of X are members of Y but some members of Y are not members of X then the members of X cannot be put in one-to-one correspondence with those of Y. Indeed, so long as X and Y are restricted to *finite* sets the principle just stated is true. But if we let X be the set of *even* natural numbers – 2, 4, 6, . . . – and Y be the set of natural numbers – 1, 2, 3, . . . – the principle is shown to be false. For although all the members of X are members of Y and some members of Y – the odd integers – are not members of X, it is not true that the members of X cannot be put in one-to-one correspondence with those of Y. What this example illustrates is that a principle which holds of all finite sets may not hold of all infinite sets. The principle underlying the second major criticism is, I have argued, such a principle.

One final point concerning my reply to the second major criticism needs to be made clear. In rejecting the principle on which the criticism rests I have contended that when a set has an *infinite* number of members, every one of which has an explanation of its existence, it *does not follow* that the existence of the set is thereby explained. In saying this I do not mean to imply that in explaining the existence of every member of an infinite set we never thereby explain the existence of the set, only that we *sometimes* do not. Specifically, we do not, I think, when we explain the existence of each member of the set by some other member of *that set*. Recall our example of M, the set of men. If we think of the members of this set forming a temporal series stretching infinitely back in time, each member's existence explained by the causal efficacy of the preceding member, we have an example, I think, in which an explanation of the existence of each member of M does not constitute an explanation of the existence of M. Let us suppose that each man is produced not by another man but by some

48

superior being, say a god. What we are supposing is that M is described as before except that instead of every member having the explanation of its existence in some preceding member of M the explanation is found in the causal efficacy of some member of the set of gods. From eternity, then, gods have been producing men. There have always been members of M and every member has an explanation of its existence. Here it does seem true to say that in explaining the existence of every member of M we have thereby explained the existence of M. If someone asks why there now are and always have been men rather than never having been any, we can say in response that there always have been men because there always have been gods producing them. This, if true, would explain why M has always had members.

In this paper I have examined two criticisms that have been advanced against that part of the Cosmological Argument which seeks to establish that not every being can be a dependent being. I have argued that each of these criticisms is mistaken and, therefore, fails as a refutation of the Cosmological Argument. If my arguments are correct, it does not follow, of course, that the Cosmological Argument is a good argument for its conclusion. But it does follow that those philosophers who have rejected the argument for either of the two criticisms discussed in this paper need to re-examine the argument and, if they continue to reject it, provide some *good* reasons for doing so.

NOTES

1. See 'The Cosmological Argument and the Principle of Sufficient Reason,' *Man and World,* **1**, No. 2.
2. Not all versions of the Cosmological Argument employ the notion of a logically necessary being. It seems likely, for example, that in Aquinas' 3rd Way the expression 'necessary being' is not used to mean a logically necessary being. (See P. Brown, St. Thomas' Doctrine of Necessary Being,' *Philosophical Review.* 73 (1964), 76–90.) But in the version we are considering it is clear that by 'necessary being' is meant a being whose existence is logically necessary. Thus Samuel Clarke, from whose work our version has been adapted, remarks: '...the only true idea of a self-existent or necessarily existing being, is the idea of a being the supposition of whose not-existing is an express contradiction.' (See Samuel Clarke, *A Demonstration of the Being and Attributes of God,* 9th edition, p. 17.) David Hume also understands the notion of a necessary being this way. Thus in his statement of the argument, which he adapted from Clarke he has Demea conclude, 'We must, therefore, have recourse to a necessarily existent being, who carries the reason of his existence in himself, and who cannot be supposed not to exist, without an express contradiction.' (*Dialogues Concerning Natural Religion,* Part IX.)

3. See, for example, Samuel Clarke's discussion of Propositions II and III in his *Demonstration*. This discussion is summarised by Hume in Part IX of his *Dialogues*.

4. 'The Existence of God, A Debate between Bertrand Russell and Father F. C. Copleston,' in John Hick (ed.), *The Existence of God* (New York: The Macmillan Company, 1964), p. 175. The debate was originally broadcast by the British Broadcasting Corporation in 1948. References are to the debate as reprinted in *The Existence of God*.

5. *Dialogues,* Part IX.

6. Samuel Clarke did not. Nor do we find Hume appealing to this inference in the course of presenting the Cosmological Argument in Part IX of the *Dialogues*.

7. Ronald W. Hepburn, *Christianity and Paradox* (London: Watts, 1958), pp. 167-68.

8. For a consideration of inferences of this sort in connection with the fallacy of composition see my paper, 'The Fallacy of Composition,' *Mind,* January 1962. For some needed corrections of my paper see Bar-Hillel, 'More on the Fallacy of Composition.' *Mind,* January 1964.

9. Of course, the three members of this collection, unlike the members of the collection of dependent beings, presumably are causally unrelated. But it is equally easy to think of collections which cannot possibly be concrete entities where members are causally related – e.g., the collection whose members are the ancestors of a given man.

10. Thus in speaking of the infinite succession, Hume has Demea say: '...and yet it is evident that it requires a cause or reason, as much as any particular object which begins to exist in time. The question is still reasonable, *why this particular succession of causes existed from eternity, and not any other succession, or no succession at all.*' (*Dialogues,* Part IX, italics mine.)

11. Debate, p. 173.

12. Paul Edwards, 'The Cosmological Argument,' in Donald R. Burrill (ed.), *The Cosmological Arguments* (New York: Doubleday & Company, Inc., 1967), pp. 113-14. Edwards' paper was originally published in *The Rationalist Annual for the Year 1939*.

QUESTIONS for further discussion:

If the foregoing version of the Cosmological argument can be defended against all difficulties, those not considered here, and those which are the topics of the paper, will its conclusion furnish ground for belief in *God*, as any actual religious believers understand 'God'? If so, how may the connection(s) between the existence of a necessary being, on the one hand, and the existence of the God of Abraham, Isaac and Jacob, the God and Father of Jesus Christ, or the one God whose prophet is Mahomet, on the other, be expressed? The corresponding question may also, of course, be raised in relation to other arguments for the existence of God, such as the Ontological argument (see above pp. 2-3) and the arguments from Design (see the following paper which, at least, touches on the question).

Paper IV
Introductory Groundwork

Notwithstanding the great influence of Hume's brief discussion of the Cosmological argument in Section IX of his *Dialogues Concerning Natural Religion*, it is to argument from Design that he devotes most of the *Dialogues*, in which one participant, Cleanthes, develops and supports one such argument, to have it subjected to the extended critique of Philo and Demea. In the following paper, Professor Swinburne disputes that the Humian critique has decisive force against arguments from Design in general, and contends that there is, importantly, another better sort of argument from Design than the one proposed by Cleanthes. This other sort, for which Swinburne is an advocate, is said to be more cogent in not being affected by some considerations which are fatal to the Cleanthes argument; and since the god whose existence the argument is held to support is not embodied, and is in immediate control from moment to moment of every event in the universe, better support is effected for (Judaeo-Christian) theism than by the rather deistic argument of Cleanthes in which God is (anthropomorphically) embodied, and may, for all the argument shows, be now disinterested in his creation, or even dead.

That Cleanthes represented views widespread among the educated in the early eighteenth century, and prompted by seventeenth century science, is clear; Deism, indeed, in its characteristic denial that God intervenes in the world *consists* centrally of the views of Cleanthes together with the denial of all, in addition to or qualification of those views, that, in Judaeo-Christian traditions, is ascribed to Revelation. Hume, therefore, attacks Deistic argument for the existence of God.

It is less clear that more orthodox theologians are so directly his targets. Butler certainly relied on some argument by analogy as does Cleanthes, and insofar as Hume urges caution about such argument, we are being cautioned about Butler. But whereas Cleanthes' analogy-argument is, first, for God's very existence, as well as to establish his attributes, Butler's is concerned only with the divine attributes, and it is not clear what is *his* ground for belief in God's existence. Berkeley's ground for belief in God's existence is nearer to Swinburne's argument than to that of Cleanthes, because the order from which Berkeley argues[1] is in part the order of a world patterned in its passage through time in accordance with natural laws.

In the twentieth century Russell does engage in brief criticism of argument based on this kind of order,[2] order of succession, in Swinburne's phrase, but much consideration of arguments from Design has followed Hume both in its particular target and in the arguments employed.[3]

To speak, as it is conventional to do, of arguments 'from Design', has suggested begging of the question, in that the *starting* point, by being described as '... Design', (rather than, say, '... order' or even '... the universe as we find it') has built into its description by us, the implication that it *has* a designer. If, instead, we describe our starting point as '... observed order in the universe', and conclude that this order is to be accounted for by postulating that it was designed, which entails that it had a designer, then the appearance of question-begging is avoided, and the argument is fairly represented. It ought, perhaps, to be called the argument to Design. One rationale for the standard usage is that the argument's starting point turns out, at the conclusion of the whole argument, to be not just order, but design. Swinburne seeks to avoid the imputation of question-begging by saying that as he uses 'design' it is not part of the word's meaning, is not analytic, that what has design has a designer, but must be established by the sort of argument he deploys. Even if Swinburne's way of avoiding the appearance of question-begging seems strained, it will be plain enough that in the argument itself no question-begging of this sort occurs.

NOTES

1. I am referring here to Berkeley's argument in *Alciphron*.
2. *Why I am not a Christian*. London, 1957. ch. 1, section entitled 'The Natural Law Argument'.
3. One writer who offers an argument from Design differing from any touched on here is Richard Taylor. See his *Metaphysics*. Englewood Cliffs, New Jersey, 1963. Pp. 94 ff.

The Argument from Design

R. G. SWINBURNE

The object of this paper[1] is to show that there are no valid formal objections to the argument from design, so long as the argument is articulated with sufficient care. In particular I wish to analyse Hume's attack on the argument in *Dialogues Concerning Natural Religion* and to show that none of the formal objections made therein by Philo have any validity against a carefully articulated version of the argument.

The argument from design is an argument from the order or regularity of things in the world to a god or, more precisely, a very powerful free non-embodied rational agent, who is responsible for that order. By a body I understand a part of the material Universe subject, at any rate partially, to an agent's direct control, to be contrasted with other parts not thus subject. An agent's body marks the limits to what he can directly control; he can only control other parts of the Universe by moving his body. An agent who could directly control any part of the Universe would not be embodied. Thus ghosts, if they existed, would be non-embodied agents, because there are no particular pieces of matter subject to their direct control, but any piece of matter may be so subject. I use the word 'design' in such a way that it is not analytic that if anything evinces design, an agent designed it, and so it becomes a synthetic question whether the design of the world shows the activity of a designer.

The argument, taken by itself, as was admitted in the *Dialogues* by Cleanthes the proponent of the argument, does not show that the designer of the world is omnipotent, omniscient, totally good, etc. Nor does it show that he is the God of Abraham, Isaac, and Jacob. To make these points further arguments would be needed. The isolation of the argument from design from the web of Christian apologetic is perhaps a somewhat unnatural step, but necessary in order to analyse its structure. My claim is that the argument does not commit any

53

formal fallacy, and by this I mean that it keeps to the canons of argument about matters of fact and does not violate any of them. It is, however, an argument by analogy. It argues from an analogy between the order of the world and the products of human art to a god responsible for the former, in some ways similar to man who is responsible for the latter. And even if there are no formal fallacies in the argument, one unwilling to admit the conclusion might still claim that the analogy was too weak and remote for him to have to admit it, that the argument gave only negligible support to the conclusion which remained improbable. In defending the argument I will leave to the objector this way of escape from its conclusion.

I will begin by setting forward the argument from design in a more careful and precise way than Cleanthes did.

There are in the world two kinds of regularity or order, and all empirical instances of order are such because they evince one or other or both kinds of order. These are the regularities of copresence or spatial order, and regularities of succession, or temporal order. Regularities of copresence are patterns of spatial order at some one instant of time. An example of a regularity of copresence would be a town with all its roads at right angles to each other, or a section of books in a library arranged in alphabetical order of authors. Regularities of succession are simple patterns of behaviour of objects, such as their behaviour in accordance with the laws of nature – for example, Newton's law of gravitation, which holds universally to a very high degree of approximation, that all bodies attract each other with forces proportional to the product of their masses and inversely proportional to the square of their distance apart.

Many of the striking examples of order in the world evince an order which is due both to a regularity of copresence and to a regularity of succession. A working car consists of many parts so adjusted to each other that it follows the instructions of the driver delivered by his pulling and pushing a few levers and buttons and turning a wheel to take passengers whither he wishes. Its order arises because its parts are so arranged at some instant (regularity of copresence) that, the laws of nature being as they are (regularity of succession) it brings about the result neatly and efficiently. The order of living animals and plants likewise results from regularities of both types.

Men who marvel at the order of the world may marvel at either or both of the regularities of copresence and of succession. The men of the eighteenth century, that great century of 'reasonable religion', were struck almost exclusively by the regularities of copresence. They marvelled at the design and orderly operations of animals and plants; but since they largely took for granted the regularities of succession, what struck them about the animals and plants, as to a lesser extent about machines made by men, was the subtle and coherent arrangement of their millions of parts. Paley's *Natural Theology* dwells mainly on details of comparative anatomy, on eyes and ears and muscles and bones arranged with minute precision so as to operate with high efficiency, and Hume's Cleanthes produces the same kind of examples: 'Consider, anatomise the eye, survey its structure and contrivance, and tell me from your own feeling, if the idea of a contriver does not immediately flow in upon you with a force like that of sensation'.[2]

Those who argue from the existence of regularities of copresence other than those produced by men, to the existence of a god who produced them are however in many respects on slippery ground when compared with those who rely for their premises on regularities of succession. We shall see several of these weaknesses later in considering Hume's objections to the argument, but it is worth while noting two of them at the outset. First, although the world contains many striking regularities of copresence (some few of which are due to human agency), it also contains many examples of spatial disorder. The uniform distribution of the galactic clusters is a marvellous example of spatial order, but the arrangement of trees in an African jungle is a marvellous example of spatial disorder. Although the proponent of the argument may then proceed to argue that in an important sense or from some point of view (e.g. utility to man) the order vastly exceeds the disorder, he has to argue for this in no way obvious proposition.

Secondly the proponent of the argument runs the risk that the regularities of copresence may be explained in terms of something else by a normal scientific explanation[3] in a way that the regularities of succession could not possibly be. A scientist could show that a regularity of copresence R arose from an apparently disordered state D by means of the normal operation of the laws of nature. This would not entirely 'explain away' the regularity of copresence, because the proponent of this argument from design might then argue that the apparently disordered state D really had a latent order, being the kind of state which, when the laws of nature operate, turns into a manifestly ordered one. So long as only few of the physically possible states of apparent disorder were states of latent order, the existence of many states of latent order would be an important contingent fact which could form a premiss for an argument from design. But there is always the risk that scientists might show that most states of apparent disorder were states of latent order, that is, that if the world lasted long enough considerable order must emerge from whichever of many initial states it began. If a scientist showed that, he would have explained by normal scientific explanation the existence of regularities of copresence in terms of something completely different. The eighteenth-century proponents of the argument from design did not suspect this danger and hence the devasting effects of Darwin's Theory of Evolution by Natural Selection on those who accepted their argument. For Darwin showed that the regularities of copresence of the animal and plant kingdoms had evolved by natural processes from an apparently disordered state and would have evolved equally from many other apparently disordered states. Whether all regularities of copresence can be fully explained in this kind of way no one yet knows, but the danger remains for the proponent of an argument from design of this kind that they can be.

However, those who argue from the operation of regularities of succession other than those produced by men to the existence of a god who produces them do not run into either of these difficulties. Regularities of succession (other than those produced by men) unlike regularities of copresence, are all-pervasive. Simple natural laws rule almost all successions of events. Nor can regularities of succession be given a normal scientific explanation in terms of something else. For the normal scientific explanation of the operation of a regularity of succession is in terms of the operation of a yet more general regularity of succession. Note too that a normal scientific explanation of the existence of regularities of copresence in terms of something different, if it can be provided, is explanation in terms of regularities of succession.

For these reasons the proponent of the argument from design does much better to rely for his premiss more on regularities of succession. St. Thomas Aquinas, wiser than the men of the eighteenth century, did just this. He puts forward an argument from design as his fifth and last way to prove the existence of God, and gives his premiss as follows:

'The fifth way is based on the guidedness of nature. An ordered-ness of action to an end is observed in all bodies obeying natural laws, even when they lack awareness. For their behaviour hardly ever varies, and will practically always turn out well; which shows that they truly tend to a goal, and do not merely hit it by accident.'[4] If we ignore any value judgment in 'practically always turn out well', St. Thomas' argument is an argument from regularities of succession.

The most satisfactory premiss for the argument from design is then the operation of regularities of succession other than those produced by men, that is, the operation of natural laws. Almost all things almost always obey simple natural laws and so behave in a strikingly regular way. Given the premiss, what is our justification for proceeding to the conclusion, that a very powerful free non-embodied rational agent is responsible for their behaving in that way? The justification which Aquinas gives is that 'Nothing . . . that lacks awareness tends to a goal, except under the direction of someone with awareness and with understanding; the arrow, for example requires an archer. Everything in nature, therefore is directed to its goal by someone with understanding and this we call "God".'[5] A similar argument has been given by many religious apologists since Aquinas, but clearly as it stands it is guilty of the grossest *petitio principii*. Certainly *some* things which tend to a goal, tend to a goal because of a direction imposed upon them by someone 'with awareness and with understanding'. Did not the archer place the arrow and pull the string in a certain way the arrow would not tend to its goal. But whether *all* things which tend to a goal tend to a goal for this reason is the very question at issue and that they do cannot be used as a premiss to prove the conclusion. We must therefore reconstruct the argument in a more satisfactory way.

The structure of any plausible argument from design can only be that the existence of a god responsible for the order in the world is a hypothesis well confirmed on the basis of the evidence, viz. that contained in the premiss which we have now stated, and better confirmed than any other hypothesis. I shall begin by showing that there can be no other possible explanation for the operation of natural laws than the activity of a god and then see to what extent the hypothesis is well confirmed on the basis of the evidence.

Almost all phenomena can, as we have seen, be explained by a normal scientific explanation in terms of the operation of natural laws on preceding states. There is however one other way of explaining natural phenomena, and that is explaining in terms of the rational choice of a free agent. When a man marries Jane rather than Anne, becomes a solicitor rather than a barrister, kills rather than shows mercy after considering arguments in favour of each course, he brings about a state of the world by his free and rational choice. To all appearances this is an entirely different way whereby states of the world may come about than through the operation of laws of nature on preceding states. Someone may object that it is necessary that physiological or other scientific laws operate in order for the agent to bring about effects. My answer is that certainly it is necessary that such laws operate in order for effects brought about directly by the agent to have ulterior consequences. But unless there are some effects which the agent brings about directly without the operation of scientific laws acting on preceding physical states bringing them about, then these laws and states could fully explain the effects and there would be no need to refer in explaining them to the rational choice of an agent. True, the apparent freedom and rationality of the human will *may* prove an illusion. Man may have no more option what to do than a machine and be guided by an argument no more than is a piece of iron. But this has never yet been shown and, in the absence of good philosophical and scientific argument to show it, I assume, what is apparent, that when a man acts by free and rational choice, his agency is the operation of a different kind of causality from that of scientific laws. The free choice of a rational agent is the only way of accounting for natural phenomena other than the way of normal scientific explanation, which is recognised as such by all men and has not been reduced to normal scientific explanation.

Almost all regularities of succession are due to the normal operation of scientific laws. But to say this is simply to say that these regularities are instances of more general regularities. The operation of the most fundamental regularities clearly cannot be given a normal scientific explanation. If their operation is to receive an explanation and not merely to be left as a brute fact, that explanation must therefore be in terms of the rational choice of a free agent. What then are grounds for adopting this hypothesis, given that it is the only possible one?

The grounds are that we can explain some few regularities of succession as produced by rational agents and that the other regularities cannot be explained except in this way. Among the typical products of a rational agent acting freely are regularities both of copresence and of succession. The alphabetical order of books on a library shelf is due to the activity of the librarian who chose to arrange them thus. The order of the cards of a pack by suits and seniority in each suit is due to the activity of the card player who arranged them thus. Among examples of regularities of succession produced by men are the notes of a song sung by a singer or the movements of a dancer's body when he performs a dance in time with the accompanying instrument. Hence knowing that some regularities of succession have such a cause, we postulate that they all have. An agent produces the celestial harmony like a man who sings a song. But at this point an obvious difficulty arises. The regularities of succession, such as songs which are produced by men, are produced by agents of comparatively small power, whose bodies we can locate. If an agent is responsible for the operation of the laws of nature, he must act directly on the whole Universe, as we act directly on our bodies. Also he must be of immense power and intelligence compared with men. Hence he can only be somewhat similar to men having, like them, intelligence and freedom of choice, yet unlike them in the degree of these and in not possessing a body. For a body, as I have distinguished it earlier, is a part of the Universe subject to an agent's direct control, to be contrasted with other parts not thus subject. The fact that we are obliged to postulate on the basis of differences in the effects differences in the causes, men and the god, weakens the argument. How much it weakens it depends on how great these differences are.

Our argument thus proves to be an argument by analogy and to exemplify a pattern common in scientific inference. As are caused by Bs. A*s are similar to As. Therefore – given that there is no more satisfactory explanation of the existence of A*s – they are produced by B*s similar to Bs. B*s are postulated to be similar in all respects to Bs except in so far as shown otherwise, viz. except in so far as the dissimilarities between As and A*s force us to postulate a difference. A well-known scientific example of this type of inference is as follows. Certain pressures (As) on the walls of containers are produced by billiard balls (Bs) with certain motions. Similar pressures (A*s) are produced on the walls of containers which contain not billiard balls but gases. Therefore, since we have no better explanation of the existence of the pressures, gases consist of particles (B*s) similar to billiard balls except in certain respects – e.g. size. By similar arguments scientists have argued for the existence of many unobservables. Such an argument becomes weaker in so far as the properties which we are

59

forced to attribute to the B*s because of the differences between the As and the A*s become different from those of the Bs. Nineteenth-century physicists postulated the existence of an elastic solid, the aether, to account for the propagation of light. But the way in which light was propagated turned out to have such differences (despite the similarities) from the way in which waves in solids are normally propagated that the physicists had to say that if there was an aether it had very many peculiar properties not possessed by normal liquids or solids. Hence they concluded that the argument for its existence was very weak. The proponent of the argument from design stresses the similarities between the regularities of succession produced by man and those which are laws of nature and so between men and the agent which he postulates as responsible for the laws of nature. The opponent of the argument stresses the dissimilarities. The degree of support which the conclusion obtains from the evidence depends on how great the similarities are.

The degree of support for the conclusion of an argument from analogy does not however depend merely on the similarities between the types of evidence but on the degree to which the resulting theory makes explanation of empirical matters more simple and coherent. In the case of the argument from design the conclusion has an enormous simplifying effect on explanations of empirical matters. For if the conclusion is true, if a very powerful non-embodied rational agent is responsible for the operation of the laws of nature, then normal scientific explanation would prove to be personal explanation. That is, explanation of some phenomenon in terms of the operation of a natural law would ultimately be an explanation in terms of the operation of an agent. Hence (given an initial arrangement of matter) the principles of explanation of phenomena would have been reduced from two to one. It is a basic principle of explanation that we should postulate as few as possible kinds of explanation. To take a more mundane example – if we have as possible alternatives to explain physical phenomena by the operation of two kinds of force, the electromagnetic and the gravitational, and to explain physical phenomena in terms of the operation of only one kind of force, the gravitational, we ought always – *ceteris paribus* – to prefer the latter alternative. Since as we have seen, we are obliged, at any rate at present, to use explanation in terms of the free choice of a rational agent in explaining many empirical phenomena, then if the amount of similarity between the order in the Universe not produced by human agents and that produced by human agents makes it at all plausible to do so, we ought to postulate that an agent is responsible for the former as well as for the latter. So then in so far as regularities of succession produced by the operation of natural laws are similar to those produced by human agents, to postulate that a rational agent is responsible for them would indeed provide a simple unifying and coherent explanation of natural phenomena. What is there against taking this step? Simply that celebrated principle of explanation – *entia non sunt multiplicanda praeter necessitatem* – do not add a god to your ontology unless you have to. The issue turns on whether the evidence constitutes enough of a *necessitas* to compel us to multiply entities. Whether it does depends on how strong is the analogy between the regularities of succession produced by human agents and those produced by the operation of natural laws. I do not propose to assess the strength of the analogy but only to claim that everything turns on it. I claim that the inference from natural laws to a god responsible for them is of a perfectly proper type for inference about matters of fact, and that the only issue is whether the evidence is strong enough to allow us to affirm that it is probable that the conclusion is true.

Now that I have reconstructed the argument from design in what is, I hope, a logically impeccable form, I turn to consider Hume's criticisms of it, and I shall argue that all his criticisms alleging formal fallacies in the argument do not apply to it in the form in which I have stated it. This, we shall see, is largely because the criticisms are bad criticisms of the argument in any form but also in small part because Hume directed his fire against that form of the argument which used as its premiss the existence of regularities of copresence other than those produced by men, and did not appeal to the operation of regularities of succession. I shall begin by considering one general point which he makes only in the *Enquiry* and then consider in turn all the objections which appear on the pages of the *Dialogues*.

1. The point which appears at the beginning of Hume's discussion of the argument in section XI of the *Enquiry* is a point which reveals the fundamental weakness of Hume's sceptical position. In discussing the argument, Hume puts forward as a general principle that 'when we infer any particular cause from an effect, we must proportion the one to the other, and can never be allowed to ascribe to the cause any qualities but what are exactly sufficient to produce the effect.'[6] Now

it is true that Hume uses this principle mainly to show that we are not justified in inferring that the god responsible for the design of the Universe is totally good, omnipotent, and omniscient. I accept, as Cleanthes did, that the argument does not by itself lead to that conclusion. But Hume's use of the principle tends to cast doubt on the validity of the argument in the weaker form in which I am discussing it, for it seems to suggest that although we may conclude that whatever produced the regularity of the world was a regularity-producing object, we cannot go further and conclude that it is an agent who acts by choice, etc., for this would be to suppose more than we need in order to account for the effect. It is, therefore, important to realise that the principle is clearly false on our normal understanding of what are the criteria of inference about empirical matters. For the universal adoption of this celebrated principle would lead to the abandonment of science. Any scientist who told us only that the cause of E had E-producing characteristics would not add an iota to our knowledge. Explanation of matters of fact consists in postulating on reasonable grounds that the cause of an effect has certain characteristics other than those sufficient to produce the effect.

2. Two objections seem to be telescoped in the following passage of the *Dialogues*. 'When two *species* of objects have always been observed to be conjoined together, I can *infer* by custom the existence of one wherever I *see* the existence of the other; and this I call an argument from experience. But how this argument can have place where the objects, as in the present case, are single, individual, without parallel or specific resemblance, may be difficult to explain.'[7] One argument here seems to be that we can only infer from an observed A to an unobserved B when we have frequently observed As and Bs together, and that we cannot infer to a B unless we have actually observed other Bs. Hence we cannot infer from regularities of succession to an unobserved god on the analogy of the connection between observed regularities and human agents, unless we have observed at other times other gods. This argument, like the first, reveals Hume's inadequate appreciation of scientific method. As we saw in the scientific examples which I cited, a more developed science than Hume knew has taught us that when observed As have a relation R to observed Bs, it is often perfectly reasonable to postulate that observed A*s, similar to As have the same relation to unobserved and unobservable B*s similar to Bs.

3. The other objection which seems to be involved in the above passage is that we cannot reach conclusions about an object which is the only one of its kind, and, as the Universe is such an object, we cannot reach conclusions about the regularities characteristic of it as a whole.[8] But cosmologists are reaching very well-tested scientific conclusions about the Universe as a whole, as are physical anthropologists about the origins of our human race, even though it is the only human race of which we have knowledge and perhaps the only human race there is. The principle quoted in the objection is obviously wrong. There is no space here to analyse its errors in detail but suffice it to point out that it becomes hopelessly confused by ignoring the fact that uniqueness is relative to description. Nothing describable is unique under all descriptions (the Universe is, like the solar system, a number of material bodies distributed in empty space) and everything describable is unique under some description.

4. The next argument which we meet in the *Dialogues* is that the postulated existence of a rational agent who produces the order of the world would itself need explaining. Picturing such an agent as a mind, and a mind as an arrangement of ideas, Hume phrases the objection as follows: 'a mental world or Universe of ideas requires a cause as much as does a material world or Universe of objects.'[9] Hume himself provides the obvious answer to this – that it is no objection to explaining X by Y that we cannot explain Y. But then he suggests that the Y in this case, the mind, is just as mysterious as the ordered Universe. Men never 'thought it satisfactory to explain a particular effect by a particular cause which was no more to be accounted for than the effect itself.'[10] On the contrary, scientists have always thought it reasonable to postulate entities merely to explain effects, so long as the postulated entities accounted simply and coherently for the characteristics of the effects. The existence of molecules with their characteristic behaviour was 'no more to be accounted for' than observable phenomena, but the postulation of their existence gave a neat and simple explanation of a whole host of chemical and physical phenomena, and that was the justification for postulating their existence.

5. Next, Hume argues that if we are going to use the analogy of a human agent we ought to go the whole way and postulate that the god who gives order to the Universe is like men in many other respects. 'Why not become a perfect anthropomorphite? Why not assert the deity or deities to be corporeal, and, to have eyes, a nose, mouths,

ears, etc.'[11] The argument from design is as we have seen, an argument by analogy. All analogies break down somewhere; otherwise they would not be analogies. In saying that the relation of A to B is analogous to a relation of A* to a postulated B*, we do not claim that B* is in all respects like B, but only in such respects as to account for the existence of the relation and also in other respects except in so far as we have contrary evidence. For the activity of a god to account for the regularities, he must be free, rational, and very powerful. But it is not necessary that he, like men, should only be able to act on a limited part of the Universe, a body, and by acting on that control the rest of the Universe. And there is good reason to suppose that the god does not operate in this way. For, if his direct control was confined to a part of the Universe, scientific laws outside his control must operate to ensure that his actions have effects in the rest of the Universe. Hence the postulation of the existence of the god would not explain the operation of those laws: yet to explain the operation of all scientific laws was the point of postulating the existence of the god. The hypothesis that the god is not embodied thus explains more and explains more coherently than the hypothesis that he is embodied. Hume's objection would however have weight against an argument from regularities of copresence which did not appeal to the operation of regularities of succession. For one could suppose an embodied god just as well as a disembodied god to have made the animal kingdom and then left it alone, as a man makes a machine, or, like a landscape gardener, to have laid out the galactic clusters. The explanatory force of such an hypothesis is as great as that of the hypothesis that a disembodied god did these things, and argument from analogy would suggest the hypothesis of an embodied god to be more probable. Incidentally, a god whose prior existence was shown by the existence of regularities of copresence might now be dead, but a god whose existence was shown by the present operation of regularities of succession could not be, since the existence of an agent is contemporaneous with the temporal regularities which he produces.

6. Hume urges – why should we not postulate many gods to give order to the Universe, not merely one? 'A great number of men join in building a house or a ship, in rearing a city, in framing a commonwealth, why may not several deities combine in framing a world?'[12] Hume again is aware of the obvious counter-objection to his suggestion – 'To multiply causes without necessity . . . contrary to true

philosophy'.[13] He claims, however, that the counter-objection does not apply here, because it is an open question whether there is a god with sufficient power to put the whole Universe in order. The principle, however, still applies whether or not we have prior information that a being of sufficient power exists. When postulating entities, postulate as few as possible. Always suppose only one murderer, unless the evidence forces you to suppose a second. If there were more than one deity responsible for the order of the Universe, we should expect to see characteristic marks of the handiwork of different deities in different parts of the Universe, just as we see different kinds of workmanship in the different houses of a city. We should expect to find an inverse square law of gravitation obeyed in one part of the universe, and in another part a law which was just short of being an inverse square law – without the difference being explicable in terms of a more general law. But it is enough to draw this absurd conclusion to see how ridiculous the Humean objection is.

7. Hume argues that there are in the Universe other things than rational agents which bestow order. 'A tree bestows order and organisation on that tree which springs from it, without knowing the order; an animal in the same manner on its offspring.'[14] It would therefore, Hume argues, be equally reasonable if we are arguing from analogy, to suppose the cause of the regularities in the world 'to be something similar or analogous to generation or vegetation.'[15] This suggestion makes perfectly good sense if it is the regularities of copresence which we are attempting to explain. But as analogous processes to explain regularities of succession, generation or vegetation will not do, because they only produce regularities of copresence – and those through the operation of regularities of succession outside their control. The seed only produces the plant because of the continued operation of the laws of biochemistry.

8. The last distinct objection which I can discover in the *Dialogues* is the following. Why should we not suppose, Hume urges, that this ordered Universe is a mere accident among the chance arrangements of eternal matter? In the course of eternity matter arranges itself in all kinds of ways. We just happen to live in a period when it is characterised by order, and mistakenly conclude that matter is always ordered. Now, as Hume phrases this objection, it is directed against an argument from design which uses as its premiss the existence of the regularities of copresence. 'The continual motion of matter . . . in less than

infinite transpositions must produce this economy or order, and by its very nature, that order, when once established supports itself for many ages if not to eternity'.[16] Hume thus relies here partly on chance and partly on the operation of regularities of succession (the preservation of order) to account for the existence of regularities of copresence. In so far as it relies on regularities of succession to explain regularities of copresence, such an argument has, as we saw earlier, some plausibility. But in so far as it relies on chance, it does not, if the amount of order to be accounted for is very striking. An attempt to attribute the operation of regularities of succession to chance would not thus be very plausible. The claim would be that there are no laws of nature which always apply to matter; matter evinces in the course of eternity all kinds of patterns of behaviour, it is just chance that at the moment the states of the Universe are succeeding each other in a regular way. But if we say that it is chance that in 1960 matter is behaving in a regular way, our claim becomes less and less plausible as we find that in 1961 and 1962 and so on it continues to behave in a regular way. An appeal to chance to account for order becomes less and less plausible, the greater the order. We would be justified attributing a typewritten version of collected works of Shakespeare to the activity of monkeys typing eternally on eternal typewriters if we had some evidence of the existence of an infinite quantity of paper randomly covered with type, as well as the collected works. In the absence of any evidence that matter behaved irregularly at other temporal periods, we are not justified in attributing its present regular behaviour to chance.

In addition to the objections which I have stated, the *Dialogues* contain a lengthy presentation of the argument that the existence of evil in the world shows that the god who made it and gave it order is not both totally good and omnipotent. But this does not affect the argument from design which, as Cleanthes admits, does not purport to show that the designer of the Universe does have these characteristics. The eight objections which I have stated are all the distinct objections to the argument from design which I can find in the *Enquiry* and in the *Dialogues,* which claim that in some formal respect the argument does not work. As well as claiming that the argument from design is deficient in some formal respect, Hume makes the point that the analogy of the order produced by men to the other order of the Universe is too remote for us to postulate similar causes.[17] I have argued earlier that if there is a weakness in the argument it is here that it is to be found. The only way to deal with this point would be to start drawing the parallels or stressing the dissimilarities, and these are perhaps tasks more appropriate for the preacher and the poet than for the philosopher. The philosopher will be content to have shown that though perhaps weak, the argument has some force. How much force depends on the strength of the analogy.

NOTES

1. I am most grateful to Christopher Williams and to colleagues at Hull for their helpful criticisms of an earlier version of this paper.
2. David Hume, *Dialogues Concerning Natural Religion*, ed. H. D. Aitken (New York, 1948), p. 28.
3. I understand by a 'normal scientific explanation' one conforming to the pattern of deductive or statistical explanation utilised in paradigm empirical sciences such as physics and chemistry, elucidated in recent years by Hempel, Braithwaite, Popper and others. Although there are many uncertain points about scientific explanation, those to which I appeal in the text are accepted by all philosophers of science.
4. St Thomas Aquinas, *Summa Theologiae*, Ia, 2, 3. Translated by Timothy McDermott, O.P. (London, 1964).
5. *Ibid., loc. cit.*
6. David Hume, *An Enquiry Concerning Human Understanding*, ed. L. A. Selby Bigge. Second Edition, 1902, p. 136.
7. David Hume, *Dialogues Concerning Natural Religion*, ed. H. D. Aiken (New York, 1948), p. 23.
8. For this argument see also *The Enquiry*, pp. 147f.
9. *Dialogues*, p. 33.
10. *Ibid.*, p. 36.
11. *Ibid.*, p. 40.
12. *Ibid.*, p. 39.
13. *Ibid.*, p. 40.
14. *Ibid.*, p. 50.
15. *Ibid.*, p. 47.
16. *Ibid.*, p. 53.
17. See, for example, *Dialogues*, p. 18 and p. 37.

QUESTIONS for further discussion:

1. Swinburne's conception of God holds God to be a disembodied ordering mind, ordering events in the physical universe. But can what is not in space, not in principle locatable, such as a mind, have effects in the physical world? How can what lacks the required spatial properties, so to say, get a grip on the physical world, to order it? If it be said that we do not know how, but that *our* minds manage it, somehow, in controlling our bodies, the question may then become whether such a conception of a human being is defective, and for the same reason, that it postulates a quite unintelligible affecting of (and being affected by) the physical world, on the part of the non-spatially-locatable mind. At this point, we require to consider large and presently contested issues in the philosophy of Mind[1].

2. The distinction, drawn by Swinburne in his second paragraph, between what is directly controlled by a mind, and what is only indirectly controlled, raises problems when we introduce the following considerations:

(a) What counts as my body may not always be clear; so artificial limbs, or, possibly transplanted, fully functioning, limbs, may or may not be thought of as parts of my body. (And I may have useless limbs, parts of my body over which I have no control at all, except insofar as they are attached to the rest of my body, and so can be dragged around by me.) Given that the criterion for my direct control, as control over what is *my body*, is thus unclear, we must ask what is Swinburne's underlying point in making the distinction.

(b) If I have direct control over that piece of matter which is the portion of the physical world in immediate 'contact' with my mental, or spiritual, non-physical part (as the ghost example suggests), then presumably if such 'contact' takes place at all (see Question 1, above) I have direct control over some of what is in my brain, and only then indirect control by means of long physiological chains of events, over all the rest of my body. (And these regularities of succession seen in the physiological chains, are presumably maintained by God, who has direct control over all the physical universe but for the few brain components directly controlled by free non-divine agents.)

(c) As to natural usage, if I am for example inscribing an illuminated address, I may at times control my hand movements, of which I am not clearly aware, by conscious movement of my elbow. It would be natural here to say that I directly control my elbow but indirectly control my hand. If this is correct, natural usage offers no obvious help.

(d) If I have direct control over that which I can control without thinking about it, that might include my motor-car if I am a practised confident driver, but exclude my right hand when I am trying to manipulate something in a skilful way.

(a) brings out that Swinburne's principal way of drawing the distinction is not satisfactory. Suggestions (b), (c) and (d) offered as in some respects plausible, nevertheless seem so at odds with what Swinburne says, that our search for a satisfactory account of the distinction has not yet clearly been successful. For the purposes of his argument from Design, we *might* perhaps ignore the distinction in terms of one's *body* as against the rest of the physical world, and follow the hint of the ghost example taking (b) as Swinburne's real intention. How would that affect the formulation of his argument from Design, for example when he affirms an analogy between regularities of succession in the natural world, and those known to have been brought about by human ordering intelligences, such as recitations of a poem or performances of a formal dance? And if Swinburne's formulation of his argument based on the order of succession runs into problems which are, at this point, not readily surmounted, may a Design argument based on order of succession be formulated so as to avoid this problem? (Berkeley's *Alciphron*, against the background of his overall metaphysics, as presented, for example, in the *Three Dialogues*, provides a valuable starting point for such an enterprise.)

NOTE

1. See further, for example, Richard Taylor, *Metaphysics*, op. cit., and/or the collection of essays edited by A. O. Rorty, *The Identities of Persons*. Berkeley, Los Angeles, and London, 1976.

Paper V
Introductory Groundwork

Some discussion of possible claims to knowledge of God which might, in principle, be based on religious experience is found in the course of Professor Flew's paper in this volume. Professor Horsburgh carries the discussion forward, looking at criticisms which such claims have commonly encountered: that those who give reports of their own religious experiences are reporting phenomena in their own *psychologies*, and not necessarily anything outside their minds; relatedly, that there is no acceptable way of *verifying* any claim of the religious person which goes beyond the psychological report, e.g. to make a claim about experiencing *God*; that if what the person who has religious experience claims to encounter cannot be truly described by us, is ineffable, any account using the language available to us, of what is (allegedly) encountered, must be unsatisfactory, even nonsensical. These critics have shared a philosophical outlook, called empiricism, which appeals to our experience as the source of usable concepts or as that against which any significant claim to knowledge must be testable. Sometimes this experience is qualified as *sense* experience. By attending carefully to the affirmations actually made by mystical writers, and by appealing to the possibility, which these writers claim to have realised, of an enlarged experience, Horsburgh seeks to undercut what he sees, echoing an earlier writer, J. S. Mill, as 'the empiricism of one who has had little experience.'

The Claims of Religious Experience

H. J. N. HORSBURGH

At one time the believer could rest securely on religious experience. The sceptics might nibble at the doctrinal frills of his religion; but they could not touch his seamless inner garment of truth, which was freshly woven in every generation by the experience of the Church's saints, and, to a lesser extent, even by the experience of the most vacillating and sinful Christian. But in our own century the sceptics have tried to set their teeth in this seamless garment. Psychologists have carried out what are commonly thought of as damaging researches into the nature of religious experience, and more recently philosophers have joined them in making difficulties for the believer – and not only the neanderthalers of the linguistic age in philosophy (the early logical positivists), but also *Homo sapiens* at his highest power, as represented by the followers of the later Wittgenstein. It is with this recent philosophical onslaught that I am concerned in this article.

An attempt to estimate its force should be prefaced by a close study of what has actually been claimed for religious experience – particularly by the mystics, since it is with them that I am primarily concerned. But such an investigation is clearly impossible, as even the classics of Western mysticism form a literature of very considerable bulk. I shall therefore confine myself to the examination of some of the claims that might be made. These claims will be considered as they are suggested by the objections themselves.

My paper, then, has two aims: (*a*) to give a brief account of the main objections which have recently been brought against religious experience as either a source of, or as a means of confirming, religious beliefs; and (*b*) to consider what important claims they dispose of (if any). The first of these aims is rendered difficult by the fact that as the attack comes from a single school of philosophy the objections tend to run into one another. The three parts into which I divide it are therefore somewhat artificial. I shall call these (1) the psychological objection, (2) the verificationist objection, and (3) the objection from the ineffable nature of religious experience. These labels are mere conveniences: I claim no special aptness for them.

I

The psychological objection is the most popular at the present time. One can therefore find many accounts of it. I shall quote from three writers who have recently put it forward. '... I want to argue', says Mr. Alasdair MacIntyre, 'that neither feeling-states nor mental images could provide evidence for religious belief .... The reason for this is that the point of the experience is allegedly that it conveys information about something other than the experience, namely, about the ways of God. Now an experience of a distinctively 'mental' kind, a feeling-state or an image cannot of itself yield us any information about anything other than the experience.'[1] A much more elaborate account of the same objection is to be found in Mr. C. B. Martin's article, 'A Religious Way of Knowing'.[2] But at one place it is succinctly stated: 'The only thing that I can establish beyond correction on the basis of having certain feelings and sensations is that I have these feelings and sensations'.[3] Finally, an account of essentially the same objection is to be found in Professor R. B. Braithwaite's Arthur Eddington Memorial Lecture.[4] 'If it is maintained', says Braithwaite, 'that the *existence* of God is known by observation in the 'self-authenticating' experience of 'meeting God', the term 'God' is being used merely as part of the description of that particular experience.' At first sight this seems to be quite a different argument. But this impression is mistaken; for what Braithwaite is saying is that the term 'God' can only be used, in such contexts, as part of one's description of a particular experience, for one is only referring to one's own feelings, images, etc., and these cannot be used to establish an existential claim.

In the above I have given pride of place to MacIntyre's statement of the objection because it reveals the nature of the argument most clearly. It is also the purest form of the argument, since both the other versions contain intrusive references to other issues. (I shall have something to say about these issues later without referring back explicitly to the passages I have quoted.)

I think it must be agreed that if mystical experiences consist merely of unusual feelings or peculiar sensations or images, i.e., if they are experiences of 'a distinctively "mental" kind' in MacIntyre's sense, they do not establish the existence of God or support any belief concerning His nature. Indeed, no massive apparatus of logic is needed to appreciate this point; it might be expected to lie within the range of even a mystic's mundane intelligence. But to say that mystical experiences are any of these things is to beg the most vital question at issue, namely, the nature of mystical experience. Admittedly, mystics do frequently use the words 'feeling', 'image', and 'sensation' in connection with their experiences. But linguistic philosophers are aware that the logical topography of these terms is most involved and should therefore be the first to appreciate that mystics may sometimes use them in different senses from those illustrated by such sentences as 'I have a prickly sensation', 'I am haunted by the image of Britannia', or 'I have a numb feeling in my toe'. In fact, it is obvious that more is claimed by mystics for their experiences than is allowed by those who urge the psychological objection; they would refuse to agree that their visions are visionary in the same sense as the dagger of Macbeth, or that their moments of ecstasy or illumination are ecstatic or illuminating in the same senses as the experience of a gardener confronted by a perfect rose or of a logician suddenly conscious of an interesting distinction. And their claim to have experienced something other than bizarre or beguiling feelings is borne out by the fact that their conduct in no way resembles the conduct of those who have devoted their lives to the cultivation of such feelings.

Braithwaite and MacIntyre do not even dismiss these claims; they ignore them. And Martin summarises the psychological objection in the sentence I have quoted before he has examined them. However, he later attempts to show that the logic of such statements as 'I have direct experience of God and therefore know He exists' is 'very, very like' the logic of such admittedly psychological statements as 'I have a queer feeling and therefore know I have a queer feeling'. I shall contend that Martin is wrong in this logical assertion. But at the moment I wish to make a different point, namely that even if these statements have a similar logic one can only rule out the existential claim with assurance by falling back (as all the writers quoted do, at least implicitly) on cast-iron assertions as to the possibilities of experience. Thus Martin says;[5] 'Because "having direct experience of God" does not admit the relevance of a society of tests and checking procedures it places itself in the company of the other ways of knowing which preserve their self-sufficiency, "uniqueness", and "incommunicability" by making a psychological and not an existential claim'. In brief, the existential claim must be withdrawn. But it is quite conceivable that the world should be such that only some people can (in the empirical sense) discover certain things about it. For all that Braithwaite, MacIntyre and Martin know to the contrary this may describe the actual situation of the mystics. In other words, the existential claim can only be ruled out by applying logical distinctions (e.g., those between thoughts, feelings, sensations, images, etc.) that have arisen out of ordinary experience. But mystical experience is not ordinary experience; and therefore, it remains an open question whether the distinctions that we ordinarily make would require either to be modified or changed altogether if account were to be taken of it. There seems to be something scholastic in its rigidity about this whole mode of argument. One can imagine, for example, the plight of a present-day scientist pitchforked without books or apparatus into the middle ages and forced to engage in discussion with philosophers who applied 20th century techniques to the elucidation of 13th century speech. At every turn he would be accused of unwarrantably extending the meanings of words, using misleading analogies, falling into mislocations and distortions of logical geography, etc., etc. What could he do if these philosophers stood on their logic and refused to enlarge their experience in the way that he might suggest?[6]

But in any case it is quite wrong to speak of the logic of statements concerning religious experience as 'very, very like' the logic of psychological statements. There are several important differences. But, at the moment, so as not to trespass on the ground of the next section, I shall mention only one. This difference arises out of the fact that, whereas psychological statements are always made with the same assurance, claims based on religious experience are made with varying degrees of assurance. Thus, it does not make sense to ask: 'Is A less sure he has the sensation x than B is sure he has the sensation y?' On the other hand it makes perfectly good sense to ask: 'Which of them is the more sure that he has had direct experience of God, A or B?'

To point out further differences would be to pass on to the verificationist objection. Indeed, the psychological objection is to be regarded as a special or disguised form of the verificationist objection, in that, if subjected to sufficient scrutiny, it turns into that objection. Thus, when someone claims to have intuitive or clairvoyant powers and refuses to admit that his 'hunches' are mere feelings, images etc., we test his claims, and the retention or withdrawal of the word 'mere' turns on the results of these tests. In advancing the psychological objection, therefore, one is maintaining either that such tests have been applied to the mystic and his claims shown to be unfounded or that (as Martin suggests) no tests can be applied to him and therefore his claims *must* be unfounded.

II

Martin raises the verificationist objection in as telling a way as any when he asks: 'How do we know that someone has had direct experience of God or that we ourselves have had such an experience?' In other cases in which existential claims are made 'a whole society of tests and checking up procedures are available'; in this case, according to Martin, it does not exist. He sharpens the objection by drawing attention to two interesting possibilities. The first of these is the possibility of a full description of an alleged direct experience of God. He writes:[7] '... the theologian discourages[8] any detailed description of the required experience ("apprehension of God"). The more naturalistic and detailed the description of the required experience became, the easier would it become to deny the existential claim. One could say, "Yes, I had those very experiences, but they certainly did not convince me of God's existence". The only sure defence here would be for the theologian to make the claim analytic – "You *couldn't* have those experiences and at the same time sincerely deny God's existence".' The second possibility is that those who used to make the existential claim should cease to do so, while maintaining that their experiences have not changed. 'Perhaps they still attend church services and pray as often as they used to do, and perhaps they claim to have the same sort of experiences as they had when they were believers, but they refuse to accept the conclusion that God exists.'[9]

I want to begin what I have to say by way of comment on this objection with some remarks on the subject of self-authentication, the topic raised by the question 'How do I know that I have had direct experience of God?'

Martin and Braithwaite pay no heed to the most remarkable feature of self-authentication in religious experience, namely, that it is not self-authenticating in the same way as it has sometimes been claimed that moral intuitions are self-authenticating. Thus, if asked 'Why is murder wrong?', the ethical intuitionist would reply 'One just *knows* that it is'. This is not a slowly dawning moral perception; it is something that strikes one as soon as one thinks about it. But mystical experience does not seem to be self-authenticating in its beginnings; or, at any rate, not so self-authenticating as to be destructive of doubt. Many religious people can set themselves the question, 'Have I had direct experience of God?' and be forced to answer either 'I don't know' or 'I think so, but I'm not sure'. Only the experiences of the greatest mystics would seem to be fully self-authenticating. As I have already shown, this growth of self-authentication serves to distinguish the logic of statements about mystical experience from the logic of ordinary experiential statements. It is also important in connection with the testing of the mystic's claims, as I hope to show.

Nobody who emphasises the importance of religious experience would wish to deny that this self-authentication is mysterious; indeed, for different reasons from those of the sceptic he would wish to stress its mystery. Nevertheless, something can be said to dispose us more favourably towards it. For example, it can be pointed out, many everyday assertions are mysterious in a somewhat similar way. Thus, when looking for a friend's house one may be told: 'Keep straight on and you can't miss it'. Painfully aware of one's capacity to miss the obvious, one may fail to be reassured by this prophecy. Yet is may be justified; and when one sees one's friend's house one may appreciate why it could be made. Similarly, one must have had certain experiences to appreciate why some experiences have been called self-authenticating.

It can also be pointed out that at least an element of self-authentication attaches to many of our cognitive experiences. Thus, we may set out to look for something without knowing what it is, impelled by an indeterminate longing. Yet faced by an object, an occupation, or an activity we may instantly recognise that it is what we have been looking for. Our response to what we find guarantees that it is the true object of our search. The religious man goes in quest of God, either alone or supported by the beliefs and practices of a religious community; and he knows when he has found Him by the overwhelming religious significance of the encounter. He has met God when it is only God Whom he could have met, i.e., when he has met the Being in Whom he can find his fulfilment.[10] This may sound like the perfect vindication of the psychological objection, since it can at once be suggested either that the mystic's voyage is one of disguised self-discovery (similar to that which reaches its completion when a man suddenly discovers that what he really wants to do is to paint), or that the whole voyage is a self-deception like that of an ancient mariner setting sail in his dreams for the wonderful port that he has never visited. The response of the mystic, it will be said, is like that of the dying man to the mirage; God is the oasis that should, that must exist – that would exist if thought really had the omnipotence that children and primitives ascribe to it. But just as the ordinary romantic youth is prepared to trade in his dreams for any pretty girl of flesh and blood, discovering that his response to the pretty girl is very different from, and goes far beyond, his response to any figure of fantasy; so the overwhelming power of the mystic's final encounter argues the Presence of a Being Who is more than a figment of his own imagination. Moreover, it is not the sickly and highly emotional who, in contemplative orders, have sometimes reached the level (as they claim) of fully self-authenticating experience; the greatest mystics appear to have been eminently sane men with a handsome disrespect for the phenomena of hysteria, self-hypnosis, and the like. Nobody, for example, can read St. John of the Cross with an open mind without being checked between facile explanations. Indeed, it may be asserted more generally that one can turn to the writings of the mystics after forty years of Freudian investigation without receiving an impression of psychological naivety. In brief, the mystery of self-authentication is more than sheer mystification, and a comparison of the mystic's claims with those of a man who is pronouncing on the peculiarities of his after-images is simply fatuous.

Finally, it is instructive to consider other cases in which the hideous cry of 'Self-authentication' would echo just as deafeningly among the ivory towers of philosophy. Let us suppose that there is a community consisting of three people, A, B, and C. They are all blind but otherwise normal. Their scientific knowledge has reached a very high level so that they have been able to develop scientific aids which fulfil all the functions of eyes with a single exception. Let us now suppose that A suddenly discovers that he can see. He tries to tell B and C about his extraordinary experiences but finds them intransigently sceptical when it is discovered that his alleged new sense gives him no predictive advantages that can be appreciated by the others. Thus as his visual experience increases he can predict colour changes that they cannot predict; but they are unimpressed by these predictions, since they question the existence of colours in A's sense. (However, they discover that his alleged colour predictions are correlated with predictable changes in what we call light waves. Thereafter they are inclined to say in the manner of Braithwaite that A's colour words function as parts of his descriptions of the anomalous experiences caused by these changes.) Inevitably, A becomes a target for the psychological and verificationist objections. He then discovers that he can often make the same predictions as the others with fewer scientific aids. After protracted tests B and C agree that he can. But when he makes existential claims on the basis of his visual experiences they immediately look stern and warn him against 'self-authentication'. He insists that looking at things is itself a way of verifying that they exist and have certain properties, but this they refuse to admit; and the logic of use supports them since, in this community, verification has nothing whatever to do with seeing. I suggest that the objection to mystical experience on the ground that it is self-authenticating may be as pointless as this objection to A's 'self-authenticating' visual experiences.

The same point can be brought out by considering another case – the impact of a stranger with extraordinary clairvoyant powers on a community of normal men. P, Q, and R – the local intellectuals – are forced to admit after extensive tests that Z can describe things which are out of sight as accurately as a normal man describes things that are fully visible and close at hand. Nevertheless, they refuse to allow him to make existential claims on the basis of these powers alone, on the ground that this would mean that his clairvoyant experiences were to be regarded as self-authenticating. Z points out that he 'makes sure' before asserting anything, 'looking' again and again as a man might look at something near him; but they insist that what Z 'sees' in this way must be checked by what he and others see in the ordinary way. But surely P, Q, and R are being unreasonable? A community in which men had reliable clairvoyant powers would have a logic that permitted them to test existential and all other cognitive claims by the use of those powers. Indeed, clairvoyant perception might count for more than seeing, since it might give rise to fewer errors, e.g., those caused by the refraction of light, etc.[11]

To all this it may be objected, however, that A and Z do not claim certainty for the statements they make on the basis of their visual or clairvoyant experiences, whereas the mystic does. But such a criticism fails to distinguish between logical and empirical centainty. A and the mystic both say they are certain; but neither is making his claims analytic – as Martin suggests. Thus, the mystic does not say 'You *couldn't* have these experiences and at the same time sincerely deny God's existence'. It remains logically possible for the mystic to stop short of the existential claim. But it appears to be empirically impossible. In this it is similar to the run of everyday assertions. Thus, a man may have smelt, felt, and seen hundreds of lampreys, yet his dying words, having eaten a surfeit of them, may still be – 'there's no such animal'. This is logically possible; but in a sincere, sane man with a good knowledge of the language it is empirically impossible.

Turning now to the charge that there are no tests in the field of religious experience, I first wish to point out that one can only reasonably ask for those tests which take account of the general nature of the field in which a claim is being made. The claims that A can see, that he is less anxious as a result of psychotherapeutic treatment, that he loves B, and that he has added a column of figures correctly are all different in important ways; and therefore the procedures by which they are tested must also be significantly different. Philosophers, in recent times, have often been unreasonable in what they have said about verification, insisting on paradigm procedures that they knew to be inapplicable to the field in which certain claims had been made. Some, for example, impugned the objectivity of history because its hypotheses could not be shown to be objective in the same ways, or in the same sense, as the hypotheses of science. But history was too respectable a study to be safely attacked for long, particularly by those with the built-in conventionality which comes from basing oneself on the ordinary usages of language. Religion has therefore become a popular object of old-style attack – even although nobody has ever supposed that the methods of verification used in scientific work can also be used to test religious claims.

But are there any tests whatsoever in the field of religious experience? In my view there are. Something can be done to understand these tests by returning to A, B and C. A is clearly extending the meaning of the term 'exist' when he claims that it should have no closer connections with what we hear than with what we see. He is unimpressed by C's ingenious objections to this extension, knowing that they represent 'the empiricism of one who has had little experience'.[12] Let us now suppose that the blindness of A, B and C has been due to some psychological disorder and that A does not suddenly develop the power of sight but accidentally undergoes some mildly therapeutic experience as a result of which he manages to detect the faintest glimmerings of light. He then slowly develops a therapeutic technique which eventually enables him to achieve normal vision. B and C can now test A's claims by using the technique that A has developed. With his assistance they may also improve it, so that, if we now suppose the community to be a larger one in which this form of blindness is endemic, a greatly improved therapeutic technique may eventually come into general use. Much may also be learnt about the stages in which correct vision is developed and the steps which have to be taken to ensure that misleading visual phenomena, such as 'seeing stars', etc., are not cultivated instead of those which A, and other competent judges, know to be desirable.

The position of the mystic is somewhat similar to A's. His claims can only be tested if others, observing the changes in him or recognising that he has travelled further along the same road as themselves, are induced to follow him. But following the mystic is a very much more complex and arduous undertaking than following A. To begin with, he insists that the religious quest is one in which progress is only made by those who give it pride of place in their lives. It therefore involves a commitment with pervasive and sometimes distasteful implications. Furthermore, one requires to have faith not only in those things which bear some resemblance to a technique, i.e., religious exercises and forms of worship, but also in the creeds and codes of behaviour which are also deemed essential.[13] It is not to be wondered at, therefore, that few who live outside the religious communities make a sustained and intensive effort to test these claims. Within the religious communities, on the other hand, they have been continuously tested over the centuries, and the stages through which the believer must pass – which vary with the nature of his religious gifts, etc. – have been very fully charted in relation to his goal. At the same time, experience has exposed the pitfalls and cul-de-sacs which he must avoid and the dangerous places where he must travel with special care. As a result, a spiritual director can make confident judgments regarding the extent and depth of the experience of those whom it is his duty to guide, basing them partly on what they have to tell him about their religious life and partly on how they behave.

All this would seem to be a perfectly adequate system of testing –

one that can be studied in a very extensive literature which shows a continuous interest in, and awareness of, the problems of verification.

NOTE. There are other points which I might make about testing that I do not feel justified in elaborating in this paper. The most important of these is that verification is affected not only by the nature of the field in which claims are to be tested but also by the dominant concepts and interests of the society in which they are made. The whole subject is therefore much more complex than it has sometimes been made to seem in the more parochial pronouncements of the logical positivists and their successors.

III

The objection which bases itself on the ineffable or inexpressible nature of religious experience is even more important than it is common, not least because the mystics and their followers are concerned to stress the same facts as the critics and sceptics. The objection is as trenchantly stated by A. J. Ayer as by any other contemporary writer. '.... To say that something transcends the human understanding', he writes, 'is to say that it is unintelligible. And what is unintelligible cannot be significantly described .... If one allows that it is impossible to define God in intelligible terms, then one is allowing that it is impossible for a sentence both to be significant and to be about God. If a mystic admits that the object of his vision cannot be described, then he must also admit that he is bound to talk nonsense when he describes it.'[14]

It would seem to be obvious that this objection is likely to have more force against some claims than against others. I propose briefly to consider its impact on the following sorts of claims so far as they rest on religious experience:

(i) That God exists.

(ii) That God has certain attributes.

(iii) That one's religious experiences provide one with reasons for conceiving God in certain ways rather than in others.

The objection strikes at the second sort of claim with greater force than at either of the others. In fact, at first sight it seems quite fatal to claims of this kind. But a second look may dispose one to think otherwise. Thus, it might be maintained that such claims are risky but possible inductions. Consider A's claim that B loves him. 'What makes you think so?' someone asks. 'Because with her I've felt – well, I can't describe it.' 'If you can't describe it, how does it help?' 'But thats just it – you can be sure when you feel like that that they really love you.' It might be said that the claim that God loves us is founded on experience in just the same way as A's claim. But such an answer is inadmissible since it overlooks the fact that A can only use his indescribable feelings as a test of B's love because there are many women and he has been able to establish the reliability of this test by first using other tests of women's feelings for him. The mystic cannot make such inductions, first, because there is only one God, and secondly because, *ex hypothesi,* he has no non-experimental methods of establishing God's love for him.

But what if it should be said – perhaps by someone who recalls the abundance of negations in the writings of the mystics – that ineffable experiences may be negative guides to what something is like? Suppose we say that the position of the mystic is similar to that of B when something brushes against her in the darkness and she finds she cannot describe it. 'Did it seem hard?' A asks. 'No.' 'Then did it seem soft?' 'No, it didn't seem soft either. Oh, I can't describe it. It just felt – funny.' But while such cases show that one can reject a description without being able to offer another in its place, one's disavowals are useless if they extend to every possible description – and it is certainly the case that the mystic refuses to accept any description of his experiences. (He writes about them in ways which prove to be evocative to his fellow mystics.) Therefore, this defence must also be rejected. However, experiences such as B's are useful because they help to remind us that when one says that x is indescribable one is not saying that it is featureless; for that which cannot be described may still be recognised when it recurs. Thus, although mystics insist that their experiences are ineffable they do classify them to some extent and are sometimes prepared to say that they have had a certain kind of experience a definite number of times.

It seems, therefore, that the ineffable character of mystical experience rules out claims of the second kind. But I fail to see how it can be used against the assertion that God exists. As I have already tried to show, experience may give us sufficient warrant for extending the meaning of the word 'exist' (or any other word); and even in ordinary life existential claims are made when one cannot describe what it is that one is affirming the existence of. Thus, when B says 'something bumped into me', she will not withdraw the existential claim when she finds she can neither identify the object nor accept any suggested description of it. But to make such a comparison is calculated to stir the critic. 'Yes', he may say, 'B persists in making an existential claim. But she only does so – and other people are only interested in her claim – because she thinks that something unidentified is present and wished to enlist other people's assistance in identifying it, lest it should prove to be dangerous or otherwise important. If, after repeated efforts, it cannot be identified she will either withdraw the existential claim or say combatively, "Well, I know that *something* bumped into me". In either case other people will cease to take an interest in it; and if B often has such experiences they will quickly come to the conclusion that she is mentally deranged. The mystic, on the other hand, is asserting the existence of something and at the same time insisting that it cannot be identified. This is very different.' Much of what I am supposing the critic to say about B's experience seems to me sound. But he is neglecting certain possibilities. Thus, it might transpire that other people had had experiences similar to B's when walking in the same locality and that in no case had it been found possible to identify what it was that bumped into them. In such circumstances an existential claim might continue to be made without any description being given of what it is that is being asserted to exist. 'But', I will be told, 'this claim will only be made for the same reason as before, namely, the possibility that further investigation will uncover the nature of this mysterious something-or-other. If no amount of investigation serves to advance our knowledge the claim will be withdrawn and the experience will be regarded as of a "distinctively mental kind".' I should agree that this is the probable course of events; but I should want to stress its unsatisfactoriness. However, even if one ignores this unsatisfactoriness an alternative remains, namely, that which is embodied in the mystic's claims. Thus, it might be found that the unknown x, which bumps into people, eludes description not because it cannot be identified but because it can only be identified in a special way. This is what mystics have said about God. Thus, it is not pointless for them to say that God exists even when they admit that He cannot be described, since they also affirm that He can be apprehended in a special way by those who seek Him. Of course, one can rule out the special non-conceptual form of apprehension spoken of by mystics as nonsensical. But if one does one is denying the meaningfulness and appositeness of an expression without having had the experiences which give it meaning and establish its appositeness – a procedure that puts one in reach of the criticism which J. S. Mill levelled at Bentham.

Again, I do not think the objection has any force against claims of the third kind, e.g., against the claim that it is best to think of God as a loving God. The mystic, in his highest spiritual flights, does not require a conception of God: at such times (if we believe him) he enjoys direct communion with God, and the special form of consciousness to which he has attained is one that has no use for concepts. But for the ordinary course of his life, and for the instruction of others, the mystic requires a conception of God. Clearly, it is a good reason for conceiving God in this way rather than in that, that it has been found that this way is the more conducive to spiritual progress, i.e., to more profound and indubitable encounters with God. Of the conceptions and descriptions that are the most useful of all it can be said that they are as true as truth can be, the point of this unfashionable statement being that they are the best spiritual ladders available, but that one comes to the end of the longest ladder and must therefore eventually discard them. Ayer simply ignores the possibility of claims of this kind.

In my view, therefore, the force of the objection which Ayer raises depends on the nature of the claim against which it is directed. It is as fatal to claims of the second variety as it is harmless when brought against claims of the first and third. But it is these latter sorts of claims which are vital to mysticism. Claims of the sort which cannot be sustained in the face of this attack are precisely the sort of claims which are clearly inconsistent with even the most obvious and familiar features of mysticism.

It has become obvious that I do not think the recent philosophical critics of mysticism have succeeded in dislodging the believer from what I take to be his ultimate stronghold. But I recognise that any rebuttals are most unlikely to convince those who are not sympathetically inclined towards mysticism. This is partly due to such factors as my own intellectual deficiencies. But it is also due to the difficulty of bringing critic and believer into effective touch with one another. One feels this in the course of reading even *New Essays in Philosophical Theology*, although the contributors (Christian and non-Christian) have a common philosophical method; and it is still more obviously true when the believer is either a mystic or one who follows him from afar. In such a case the critic is like an elephant, the believer like a whale, and their combat is apt to have the unreality of a schoolboy frolic in which 'dead' and 'living' dispute as to which is which. In a disagreement of this kind there must come a point when the whale can only tempt the elephant by hinting at the marvels of underwater life, and the elephant can only stamp his feet, indicating that it is he who stands on solid ground. But there is a vital difference between them; for Leviathan, the father of the whales, will only be found – if he is found at all – by those who venture from the land.

NOTES

1. *New Essays in Philosophical Theology*, pp. 255-256.
2. *Mind*, 1952; reprinted in *New Essays*, pp. 76-95.
3. *New Essays*, p. 79.
4. *An Empiricist's View of the Nature of Religious Belief*, p. 4.
5. *New Essays*, p. 85.
6. The cult of failing to understand one's opponents has reached such proportions in some quarters that it gives rise to curious flickers of apprehension. Thus, I have never heard a philosopher complain that he cannot understand those stories of Edgar Allan Poe's in which the spirit of someone dead returns to inhabit or share the body of someone living. Yet in discussions of immortality many philosophers fail to understand similar notions. One can only grieve when the hallmark of philosophical acumen becomes an incapacity to understand.
7. *New Essays*, p. 80.
8. Martin produces no evidence whatsoever to justify the use of the word 'discourage'. This would seem a peculiarly disingenuous attack, coming from one who would probably also wish to urge the objection from the ineffable nature of mystical experience.
9. *New Essays*, p. 87.
10. As P. T. Geach says, 'in "God exists" we are not predicating something of God, but predicating the term "God" itself; "God exists" means "something or other is God" '. See *Proceedings of the Aristotelian Society*, 1954-55, p. 266.
11. To this it might be objected that my use of the word 'reliable' refers back to such tests as creatures like myself are able to employ. But this criticism misses a big point in order to make a small one. The big point is that one's native constitution might be such that clairvoyance provided one with part of one's criteria of reliability.
12. J. S. Mill's criticism of Bentham. See *Mill on Bentham and Coleridge*, p. 62.
13. The 'experiment' has certain features which are not fully paralleled in any other. Thus, one has to commit oneself not only to making a certain experiment but to believing that it will have a certain outcome; one must have faith in the mystic and in the God Whom he is inviting one to seek. Of course, men have often staked their lives on the result of an experiment. But the same experiment might

have been successfully conducted – or another experiment designed to test the same claims – with less at stake. When the stakes are less than this in the religious experiment its results are invariably negative. Some 'experiments' in the field of human relations are somewhat similar. I am indebted to Mr. Arthur Burns for stressing this vital difference to me in discussion.

14. *Language, Truth, and Logic,* 2nd Edition, p. 118.

QUESTIONS for further discussion:

Suppose that human knowledge of God is only to be had by the kind of mystical experience of which this paper speaks. How then ought someone to respond who has not himself had this sort of mystical experience, but who is confronted by mystical writings? Ought he to accept their testimony, or ought he to try to share their acquaintance–knowledge of God? Is it reasonable for him to attempt this latter unless he *does* accept their testimony? Is it possible for him reasonably to accept their testimony unless he *has* come to share this acquaintance–knowledge of God? If someone would try to share the mystics' acquaintance–knowledge of God, what conditions, if any, should he set out to satisfy? What if amongst the conditions predisposing one to have such experience, is the love of God?

What are the implications for religious *doctrines*? Can religious teaching about God be affirmed as true? If not, what *will* be the role and purpose of language which religious teachers and preachers use?

Paper VI
Introductory Groundwork

Religious experiences have been given explanations in quite non-theistic terms. So adolescent glandular activity, creative human transfiguration of memories, and a variety of psycho-analytical accounts of religious experiences have been offered, altogether leaving God out of the account. The further step is then taken, sometimes explicitly, sometimes unexpressed, taken for granted, that since the favoured natural explanation of the experience is acceptable, this experience cannot be an experience of God. It is this further step which Professor Wainwright contests: even if we accept that by the standards of acceptability appropriate to natural explanations, some natural explanation of a religious experience is an adequate explanation, the question of whether the experience was an experience of God, in Professor Wainwright's view, still remains undetermined.

In view of this contention of Professor Wainwright it is worth asking *why* the acceptance of a natural explanation of an experience *should* have been thought to rule out the contention that God is experienced. Perhaps the explanation lies in the confusing of these two questions:

1. If an experience has a natural explanation, may it be an experience of God?
2. If an experience has a natural explanation, *need* we explain this experience as an experience of God?

Question (2) is likely to arise in (apologetic) discussion where the *challenge* is thrown out, by the religious believer, to explain what seems to the believer a religious experience in non-theistic terms; it is implied that failure to do so renders a theistic account of the matter more cogent. Naturalistic accounts and theistic accounts are, on this view, and at this point, alternatives. It is not that the believer supposes the processes of nature to be generally independent of God, but rather that, confronted by non-theism which, like much non-theism regards natural processes and natural explanation as requiring no invoking of God, the believer attempts to cite a phenomenon, an allegedly religious experience, which can only be accounted for in theistic terms. If this *is* his aim, and this the dialectical context of his reference to supposedly religious experience, he will have failed if an adequate natural explanation of the experience is produced. It is perhaps easy casually to suppose that a negative answer to question 2, and the failure of the apologist's aim in respect of question 2, licenses a negative answer to question 1 also. Professor Wainwright argues to the contrary.

Natural Explanations and Religious Experience

WILLIAM J. WAINWRIGHT

1. In an essay entitled 'Psychological Explanations of Religious Belief',[1] William Alston presents the following argument (or something very much like it):

(1) If an experience of x (e.g. having visual impressions of pink elephants) is a perception of x, then x is a causally necessary condition of[2] the experience of x.

(2) If there are causally sufficient conditions for x which do not include y, then y is not a causally necessary condition of x. Therefore,

(3) If there are causally sufficient conditions for the experience of x which do not include x, then x is not a causally necessary condition of the experience of x. (From 2.) Therefore,

(4) If there are causally sufficient conditions for the experience of x which do not include x, then the experience of x is not a perception of x. (From 1 and 3.) Therefore,

(5) If there is a set of *natural* conditions which is causally sufficient for the occurrence of religious experience (an experience of God or a transcendent order, or something of the kind), then the experience is not a genuine perception of God or a transcendent order, etc. (From 4.)

In the remainder of the paper, I will examine this argument. My purpose in doing so is twofold. First, to show that even if we were to be presented with what appears to be an adequate scientific explanation of religious experience this argument could not be employed to establish the proposition that those experiences are not veridical. In the second place (though I shall not discuss this separately) the discussion as a whole suggests that the commonly accepted thesis about perception which is stated in the first premiss of our argument is not as clear as one might think, for it is not clear just how we are to

89

construe the expression 'causally necessary condition' which occurs in the consequent of that premiss.

2. The first premiss of our argument is not clearly true. If that premiss is true at all it is presumably necessarily true, but its necessity is not obvious. Suppose that we are able to produce visual impressions of a peculiar kind of table by stimulating certain areas of the brain even when no table of that kind is present, and that we stimulate (in the right way) the brain of a person who is conscious, who possesses normal vision and whose eyes are open and directed at a table of the kind in question which is located two feet away from him. The presence of that table is not a causally necessary condition of his visual impressions, for those impressions would have occurred even if the table had been absent. If it were clear that the first premiss of our argument was true in all possible circumstances then it would be clear that in the circumstances which have just been described, the subject does not see the table. This, however, is not clear.³

3. In a general way, what is wrong with this argument is clear enough. It is assumed that if there is an adequate natural· explanation of religious experience, then that experience cannot be grounded in God's causal activity. (For the argument is essentially this: if there is an adequate natural explanation of religious experience, then God isn't a cause of it, and if God isn't a cause of it then that experience cannot be a genuine perception of God.) But this assumption is not obvious and is incompatible with the theist's belief that all or most phenomenal events are such that even though adequate scientific explanations can (in principle) be provided for them, they are, none the less, grounded in God's causal activity.

Nevertheless, it must be admitted that the argument which we presented at the beginning of this paper is a plausible one, and that we do not yet know exactly what is wrong with it.

We must begin by pointing out that 'causally sufficient condition' may be used in at least two senses. In the first sense, x is a causally sufficient condition of y, if and only if given x and certain background conditions, y will occur. Thus, taking a large dose of arsenic is (in this sense) a causally sufficient condition of death, since taking a large dose of arsenic in certain familiar circumstances invariably results in death. In the second sense, x is a causally sufficient condition of y if and only if given x *alone*, y will invariably result.⁴ If x

is a causally sufficient condition of *y* in this strong sense, then it must include all the necessary conditions of *y*. (If it does not, then it will not be true that *x alone* will invariably result in *y*.) Taking arsenic is not a causally sufficient condition of death in this strong sense, since given an odd physiological constitution, or the fact that an antidote is taken in time, or something of the sort, one can take a large dose of arsenic and not die.

If 'causally sufficient condition' is construed in the first and weak sense, then the second premiss of our argument is false. As our example suggests, there are many cases in which while there are causally sufficient conditions (weak sense) for an occurrence which do not include some factor *y*, *y* is nevertheless a causally necessary condition of that occurrence. Thus, while ingesting a large quantity of arsenic is sometimes a causally sufficient condition (weak sense) of death and does not itself include the failure to take an antidote, the failure to take an effective antidote is a causally necessary condition of the deaths which result.

If 'causally sufficient condition' is taken in the second and strong sense, the prospects for the argument look brighter. If the expression is taken in this sense 2 is true, and (assuming that 1 is acceptable) the argument is sound. The conclusion, however, is now innocuous. If 'causally sufficient condition' is taken in the strong sense our conclusion is logically equivalent to:

> (5') If there is a set of natural conditions which when taken alone will invariably result in the occurrence of religous experience, then that experience is not a genuine perception of God or a transcendent order, or of anything else of that kind.

5′ (and thus 5) is innocuous because it cannot, in practice, be used to show that religious experience is not veridical. Suppose we are presented with a causal account of religious experience which is believed by the scientific community to be fully adequate. Are we entitled to infer that the experiences are not genuine perceptions of God, etc.? We are entitled to draw this conclusion on the basis of 5′ only if we have good reason to believe that the causes which are specified in that account can, when taken alone, i.e. in the absence of (among other things) any divine activity, produce the experiences in question. Without a disproof of the existence of God and other supra-empirical agents, it is totally unclear how we could ever know that this was the case.[5]

I conclude then, that if 'causally sufficient condition' must be, taken in one or the other of these two senses, then either the argument is unsound (for one of its premises is false) or, in spite of appearances, its conclusion is innocuous.

4. One final remark. At one point Professor Alston suggests that:

> (6) If an experience of *x* is a perception of *x*, not only must *x* be a cause of that experience, it must also occur 'somewhere (*not too far back*) in the chain of causes' which give rise to that experience. (My italics.)

Perhaps it is the case that if an adequate scientific explanation of religious experience can (in principle) be provided then while God's activity may be a causal condition of that experience, it cannot be anything but a remote cause of it, in which case religious experience is not veridical.

I have two comments. In the first place, I do not see why remoteness, or the lack of it, is relevant to a consideration of the veridical character of the experience whose claims are in question, i.e. I do not see why we should suppose that 6 is true. In the second place, it is by no means clear that the presence of an adequate scientific explanation of religious experience (or any other phenomenon) in any way tends to show that God is a remote cause of that experience (or phenomenon). Classical theists generally distinguish between two levels of causality, arguing that God's activity is an immediate cause of all events even though the same events are members of chains of natural causes which do not include God. It is not clear that this is nonsense. If it is not then it is entirely possible for there to be an adequate scientific account of religious experience (an account which links the occurrence of religious experience to other events on the phenomenal level and which does not, of course, mention God) even though God is an immediate cause of that experience and of each member of the chain of natural causes which leads up to it.[6]

NOTES

1. In *Faith and the Philosophers*, ed. John Hick; New York, 1964, pp. 88–90.
2. I think that this is what Professor Alston means. One might suppose that all that is necessary is that *x* be a causal condition of the experience of *x*, not that it be a *necessary*

causal condition of that experience. However, if the premiss is construed in this way, the argument loses much of its force. Other premises must be modified accordingly and while it is plausible to suppose that if there is a set of causes which does not include *y* and which is sufficient for the occurrence of an event, *x*, then *y* is not a necessary condition of that event (our second premiss), it is considerably less plausible to suppose that if there is a set of causes which does not include *y* and which is sufficient for the occurrence of *x*, then *y* is not a cause of *x*, for the effect might be overdetermined. (That there cannot be two sets of conditions for *x*, both of which are present and operating, and one or both of which are sufficient to produce *x* is, I think a mere dogma.)

3. There is another proposition which is similar to 1, which may be necessarily true, and with which it is (barely) possible that 1 is being confused, viz., that *x* must be present to one who experiences *x* if his experience of *x* is to count as a perception of *x*. This proposition does not clearly entail 1. (For one thing, though the notion of presence is vague enough (and undoubtedly varies with the type of experience which is in question) it seems reasonably clear that *x is present to y* does not entail *x is a causally necessary condition of y's experience of x*.)

4. In both cases, the biconditional is intended to be true by definition.

5. We could not, for example, remove God from existence and show that those causes still produce these effects.

6. One might suggest that the kind of causality which is involved here is not the kind which must be present if experiences of God are to count as perceptions of God. But why say this?

QUESTIONS for further discussion:

On Professor Wainwright's view it is not clear what sort of causal role, if any, that which is perceived must have in the occurrence of an experience of its being perceived. So, where it is in question what objective reality, if any, is experienced, appeals to the experience's causation will be unhelpful; how else, though, *are* we to distinguish experiences of God from experiences wrongly interpreted as being of God? In his section 4 above, Professor Wainwright attributes to (Classical) theists the view 'that God's activity is an immediate cause of all events even though the same events are members of chains of natural causes which do not include God'. In the context of this paper, clearly, events in the mind, such as experiences, are taken to be among the events of which God's activity is an immediate cause. Acquiring beliefs would presumably also be in this class of events.

Such a view has its difficulties. It appears to leave no room for the free play of creative human imagination, no room for (to take a trite example) my freely conjuring up in my mind's eye the image of a log fire, or your freely choosing to imagine what your parents' first meeting might have been like. Further, our acquisition of *erroneous* beliefs would seem on this view to be God's responsibility; and so, in particular would be an erroneous belief to the effect that a supposedly religious experience is an experience of God.

A comprehensive discussion of possible theistic explanations of erroneous belief is not possible here. But the particular case of erroneous belief that some experience is an experience of God may perhaps be accounted for in terms of the inappropriate exercise of human freedom. Imaginatively and freely to entertain an image or conception, aware that that is what you are doing, does not, of course, explain such error. But there are often thought to be many species of what is called wishful thinking, where ill-recognised by us, we generate for ourselves conceptions and images and seemingly (to us) irresistible (by us) interpretations of our experiences. *One* of the ways (formally described here, but subtly employed by the mystics) of estimating whether a person has experienced God is to investigate whether that person's will has been wayward by the criteria set out in the religious tradition for the rightly oriented will, and whether this wayward will has initiated the occurrence of the experience and/or wilfully misinterpreted the experience as an experience of God. If so, some presumption is created against the experience's being an experience of God.

What other criteria for correctly interpreting religious experiences might be employed? Might the context of the experience, or the significance of the experience for the person who has it, be invoked, and if so, how, more precisely?

Paper VII
Introductory Groundwork

What does it mean to accept theism, or Christianity, as rational? The earlier papers in this collection are concerned to discuss: (a) grounds for holding theistic or Christian *beliefs* to be *true*, or (b) reasons for thinking such *beliefs* to be *false*. And one natural view to take would be that theism or Christianity are rational if there are grounds for thinking their distinctive claims more probable than not, more probably true than not.

However the rationality of theism or Christianity *may* be regarded rather as the rationality of (the adoption of) a policy. To become a theist or a Christian will then be to set out on a policy estimated to be most worthwhile. This policy will certainly involve believing particular propositions, accepting them as true; it will also involve leading one's life in distinctive ways. The adoption of one belief/lifestyle as against another is a matter for rational evaluation; such evaluation might well be in part prudential, and there are other sorts of possible evaluations, moral, or conceivably aesthetic, evaluations, for example, which properly enter the account. In deciding which policy to adopt, estimation of the truth of theistic or Christian claims still surely has *a* place, but, as Swinburne's discussion shows in this next paper, it is conceivable that it may not be the sole, or even the weightiest, consideration in the determination of the rational policy for living our life. These other sorts of evaluation will also have an important place, on this view, in determining the rationality of theism or Christianity. Pascal discussed the rationality of becoming a Christian as an issue of this kind. Professor Swinburne seeks here to refine and amend Pascal's discussion; in so doing, he not only indicates how the discussion of the rationality of world views, on this understanding of rationality, should go, but also sets out the rationale for some prominent features of Christian proclamation and apologetic.

The Christian Wager

R. G. SWINBURNE[1]

On what grounds will the rational man become a Christian? It is often assumed by many, especially non-Christians, that he will become a Christian if and only if he judges that the evidence available to him shows that it is more likely than not that the Christian theological system is true, that, in mathematical terms, on the evidence available to him, the probability of its truth is greater than half. It is the purpose of this paper to investigate whether or not this is a necessary and sufficient condition for the rational man to adopt Christianity.

The Christian is a man who believes a series of propositions (accepts the Christian theological system as basically correct) and tries to act in a certain way (sets himself to live the Christian life). Several recent theologians have claimed that the Christian is a man who enters into a personal relationship with Christ, not a man who accepts a series of propositions. Now indeed there is more to faith than mere belief-that (Thou believest that God is one; Thou doest well: The devils also believe and shudder'. James 2.19). But, as Professor Price painstakingly pointed out[2] – belief 'in' always presupposes belief 'that'. Belief in God presupposes the belief that He exists. A man who believes in the God of the Christians must – of logical necessity – believe that a being with the defining properties of the God of the Christians exists. A man who claims to believe in God may indeed mean much more by his claim than that he believes that God exists; he will often mean that he puts his confidence in God to help in life's difficulties. But to put one's confidence in a person is something one does. Putting one's confidence in God is among the many actions to which the Christian is committed. The man who makes no effort to do any of these actions, to lead the Christian life, cannot be described as a Christian, whatever his beliefs. So the Christian is a man who believes a series of propositions and tries to act in a certain way.

The rational man is the man who pursues a policy if and only if he judges that the expected gain or mathematical expectation from it exceeds the expected gain (positive or negative) from not pursuing the policy. (If the expected gains from pursuing or not pursuing the policy are equal, the rational man may do either.) The expected gain from a policy is the sum of the values of each possible outcome of the policy, each multiplied by the probability of that outcome. The probability of some outcome O of a policy is the probability of the existence of that state of affairs under which O will be the outcome of the policy. The rational man will thus evaluate the probabilities of the existence of the different states and the value of each outcome, calculate the expected gain from pursuing or not pursuing a policy and act accordingly. Now let us suppose to start with, to simplify the picture, that the only considerations relevant are prudential ones. In that case the rational man is the prudent man, the man who pursues his long-term self-interest. Then the value of an outcome of a policy will be the amount of happiness which it brings to the agent. The rational man will seek to pursue those policies which will maximise his happiness.

Let me give a trivial example to illustrate the above points for those unfamiliar with the terms. A man is deciding between two policies – to bet £1 that Eclipse will win the Derby, or not to bet. There are two possible states of affairs – Eclipse will win, Eclipse will not win. After careful study of the form book, the man estimates the probability that Eclipse will win as 0.2 and so the probability that he will not win as 0.8. The odds offered by bookies are 6-1. Hence if the man bets there are two distinct outcomes – if Eclipse wins, he gains £6; if Eclipse loses, he loses £1. If the man does not bet, the two outcomes are identical – he neither gains nor loses. Now if the value of the outcome for him is measured by their monetary value, then the expected gain of betting is £6 × 0.2 − £1 × 0.8 = £0.4, and the expected gain of not betting is £0 × 0.2 − £0 × 0.8 = £0. Hence the man ought to bet. Of course the value of the outcomes may not be measured by their monetary value – the loss of the £1 may be as undesirable a loss as the win of £6 is a desirable gain. In that case we can represent the gain and loss both by one unit of value. In that case the expected gain of betting will be 1 × 0.2 − 1 × 0.8 = − 0.6, and the expected gain of not betting, as before, 0. Hence in that case the rational man will not bet.

Now it is well known that Pascal's claim that the rational man will become a Christian represented the rational man as choosing

97

between the policies of becoming or not becoming a Christian in this kind of way.

'Let us then examine the point and say 'God is', or 'He is not'.

But to which side shall we incline? Reason can decide nothing here.... A game is being played ... heads or tails will turn up.

What will you wager?'[3]

If you bet on God and win, you win 'an infinity of infinitely happy life';[4] whereas if you bet on God and lose, you lose a mere finite amount. If you bet on no God, or, which amounts to the same thing, refuse to bet openly, then, if you win, you gain a mere finite amount, mere temporary happiness, whereas if you lose, you obtain 'an eternity of miseries'.[5] Hence you ought to bet on God.

Our proposition is of infinite force: when there is the finite to stake in a game where there are equal risks of gain and loss, and the infinite to gain. This is demonstrable; and if men are capable of any truths this is one.'[6]

There is a lot wrong with Pascal's argument, and it is instructive to consider exactly what. I shall ignore, to begin with, the obvious theological objection that God does not consign to eternal Hell those who die non-Christians for no fault of their own. It will later appear that any mistake in describing the fate of non-Christians if the Christian theological system is true, does not necessarily upset the argument.

First, Pascal has stated the alternative states misleadingly. If the alternatives are meant to be 'there is a Christian God' and 'there is no after-life', then Pascal has ignored other possible states of affairs – e.g. 'There is a god who consigns Christians to eternal Hell and non-Christians to eternal Heaven'.[7] Alternatively, Pascal may have intended his alternative states to be simply 'There is a Christian God' and 'There is not a Christian God'. But in that case it is unclear what are the outcomes and so the gains and losses on the second alternative of the two policies – Heaven remains a possible outcome of Christian or non-Christian even on this alternative.

Now clearly we can represent the alternative states as two or many or infinite. Yet perhaps the most useful way to represent them is threefold:

(A) The God of the Christian exists.

(B) There is no after-life.

(C) There is an after-life but no Christian God.

The outcomes of the two alternative policies, becoming or not becoming Christian, are then as Pascal stated them for alternatives A and B; but there are a variety of possible outcomes under the third alternative, and we cannot say much definite about them. The outcomes under the alternative policies, however we evaluate them numerically, will be as follows:

	A	B	C
(1) Becoming Christian	Christian life of worship and service followed by eternal heaven	Christian life of worship and service	Christian life of worship and service followed by?
(2) Not becoming Christian	Worldly life followed by eternal Hell	Worldly life	Worldly life followed by?

We will indicate by A^1 the value (positive or negative) of the outcome of policy (1) under state of affairs A, and so on.

A second fault in Pascal's argument is this. Pascal assumed that all men would evaluate in the same way as he the various outcomes. But in fact, rightly or wrongly men will put very different values from each other on the different outcomes. Life in the Christian Heaven appeals to some more than others, and the life of worldly bliss enjoyed by the non-believer also appeals to some more than others. Further of course some men (e.g. the rich) have more opportunity than others to profit from the license of unbelief and so will have a gayer time in consequence. Likewise the Christian religion may demand more sacrifices of some (e.g. the rich) than of others. The different courses of action bring different gains to the twentieth-century business man and the negro in the Ghetto.

Thirdly Pascal supposes (by his remarks 'There are equal risks of gain and loss' and 'Reason can decide nothing here') that the probabilities of his two alternative states are equal. This claim is, to say the least, arguable. Most of natural theology is devoted to arguing about it. But his argument does not depend on this claim. All we need is some estimate of the probability of alternative states to get the argument off the ground, and, as will be seen, we can reach Pascal's conclusion without having his estimate of probabilities.

Now the rational action for a man will be determined by his estimates of the respective probabilities of the three alternative states and his evaluation of the outcomes under them. The difficulty is that we do not know what our fate will be, after death, if the alternative C be true. Nevertheless men may ascribe probabilities to the other alternative states and evaluate the possible outcomes in such a way that they can judge that one policy would be the best, even if they cannot estimate by how much the best. Thus they may ascribe a probability of zero to alternative C – in which case evaluation of gains and losses under it makes no difference to the calculation. Or, more likely, their scale of values may be such that they can say this much about the gains and losses under alternative C – that C_1 cannot exceed A_1 since Heaven is for them the highest possible bliss, that C_2 can only exceed A_1 by an infinitesimal amount since the maximum gain from life after death, if policy (2) be followed in state of affairs C, can at best only equal that obtained if policy (1) be followed in state of affairs A, and that the very slight difference in happiness on Earth can make very very little difference to the eternal balance sheet.

Once we have in this way assessed the probabilities of alternative states and the values of possible outcomes, we can work out expected gain under the two policies. The expected gain under policy (1) – becoming Christian will be

$$P(A).A_1 + P(B).B_1 + P(C).C_1$$

where $P(A)$ is the probability that A is true etc. If this exceeds the expected gain under policy (2)

$$P(A).A_2 + P(B).B_2 + P(C).C_2$$

we ought to become Christian; otherwise not. Our estimates will depend on how desirable we consider the different outcomes. If we have Pascal's standards, our evaluation can be represented as follows:

$A_1 = 1$	$B_1 = 0$	$1 \leqslant C_1 \leqslant -1$
$A_2 = -1$	$B_2 = 0$	$1 \leqslant C_2 \leqslant -1$

These standards are Pascal's, since for him the ratio of wordly gains and losses to gains in the life to come, if there is one, is of finite to infinite. It is more convenient for the purposes of my calculation to measure Pascal's comparative evaluations on a scale on which $A_1 = 1$, $B_1 = 0$, etc., rather than one on which $A_1 = \infty$, $B_1 =$ some finite number. However, Pascal's standards are not everyone's, and someone else might evaluate the alternatives as follows:

$A_1 = 1$ $B_1 = -0.0005$ $1 \leqslant C_1 \leqslant -1$

$A_2 = -1$ $B_2 = +0.0005$ $1 \leqslant C_2 \leqslant -1$

Then on this estimate of probabilities

$$P(A) = 0.1; \; P(B) = 0.85; \; P(C) = 0.05,$$

policy (1) ought to be followed. Yet on this estimate $P(A) = 0.0001$, $P(B) = 0.99985$, $P(C) = 0.00005$, policy (2) ought to be followed. On some estimates of probability, it will be unclear which is the rational policy because of the uncertainty of gains and losses, if C be true. In such circumstances, we ought to divide alternative C up into different possible states – e.g. Ca (After-life rewards distributed according to Hindu scheme), Cb (Christians go to Hell, non-Christians cease to exist), etc. – in such a way that we can ascribe values and probabilities, so as to get a clear indication of the best policy. I conclude that Pascal's system of evaluating whether the man concerned with his long-term interests ought to become a Christian is perfectly workable, but it does not necessarily yield Pascal's results.

Two points must now be made to tidy up the argument so far. First, Pascal's supposition that every man who dies a non-Christian goes, if the Christian God exists, to eternal Hell, would be denied by most Christians. Many Christians would say that only the culpable non-Christian goes to eternal Hell for his beliefs, whereas the man who was a non-Christian because the Christian alternative was never presented to him or because he mistakenly judged it irrational to become Christian would not go to Hell for his beliefs. However, if this is the fate of the non-Christian under alternative (A), calculations of the best policy based on this supposition will be the same as those based on the original supposition. For the investigator is a man to whom the Christian alternative has been presented and who must assume that he has not made a mistake in his calculations – hence it is irrelevant what happens to the man to whom the Christian alternative has not been presented or to the man who unintentionally miscalculates. But not all Christians believe that anyone will go to Hell. Some Christians would say that the culpable non-Christian merely ceases to exist – this supposition means that $A_2 = B_2$. This supposition may make a different policy the best one – on some estimates of value and probability. Some few Christians would maintain the rather unbiblical view that all men go to Heaven eventually – the man who follows policy (1) simply goes there sooner. On most estimates of probability and evaluations of outcomes on this supposition policy (2) would seem to come out the best. Further of course most Christians today think of Hell, not as the mediaeval place of literal fiery torment, but merely as a state of separation from God. In so far as different suppositions about the fate of the non-Christian on alternative (A) make a difference to what is the best policy, the alternative must be subdivided and probabilities and values ascribed to Aa (Christians go to eternal Heaven; non-Christians to eternal Hell), Ab (Christians go to eternal Heaven; non-Christians cease to exist) etc.

The second relevant point is this. A man who decides to become a Christian does not merely decide to act in a certain way but decides to hold certain beliefs. The convert may not have held, when wondering whether or not to become a Christian, that the Christian theological system was probably true, but in becoming a Christian he must now adopt this view. Is it logically possible for him to do so? Can a man adopt a belief? Certain philosophers from Hume[8] onwards have held that our beliefs are not subject to our control. If they are right, it cannot be rational for us to decide to become Christians, unless we are already convinced of the truth of the Christian theological system, for it cannot be rational for us to do what is not logically possible. Now there *may* be something odd about the suggestion that a man could decide to believe something. But there seems nothing odd about the suggestion that a man could decide to take certain action which had the known effect of inducing some belief.[9] A man might, for instance, adopt Pascal's own programme – take holy water, have masses said, etc.[10] Or he might say prayers; or he might just think hard about certain kinds of evidence for his proposition. Having considered the difficulty, I shall nevertheless in future, to avoid the cumbersome phrase, often speak of choosing or deciding to believe, rather than of choosing or deciding to take steps with the known effect of inducing a belief. The former expressions are now meant to be mere definitional substitutes for the latter.

So then if the rational man is the prudent man, whether or not he becomes a Christian depends on how he estimates the happiness provided by the different outcomes and how he assigns probabilities to the different alternative states. Now although we shall shortly have to think of the rational man as a less selfish person, the account so far does elucidate two features of Christian apologetic which have been ignored by most philosophers of religion.

The first is that the Christian preacher to the unconverted is often concerned not with proving the Christian religion to be true, but with expounding what it teaches and the new relationship to God and his fellows which the Christian believes that he and only he will enjoy now and hereafter. An extreme form of this kind of preaching, more fashionable in the past than now, was the sermon which contrasted the joys of Heaven with the pains of Hell, and exhorted men to pursue the good life lest they find themselves in Hell forever after death. Another form of such preaching is the sermon which tells of the joy of Christians on Earth and contrasts it with the dreariness of the non-Christian life on Earth. Many sophisticated philosophers of religion would pour scorn on preaching of this kind. What matters, they would urge, is not what the Christian system offers or threatens, but whether or not it is true, and if the preacher is not prepared to produce evidence to show this, his talk is mere rhetoric. If my argument is correct, such philosophers would not be sophisticated enough. What the preacher has been trying to do is to persuade men of the desirability of what the Christian religion offers here and hereafter, and thereby to show it to be rational for men to gamble all to gain it. In so far as the preacher makes men give a higher value to A_1 *and a lower value to* A_2, then for fixed $P(A)$, he makes it more rational for men to become Christian. The more desirable is Heaven and the less desirable is Hell the more sensible it is to risk much to get to Heaven and avoid Hell, for any given probability that the Christian system is true. Further, in telling of the joy of the Christian life and the dreariness of the non-Christian life on Earth the preacher is presenting an immensely powerful argument for becoming Christian. For he is claiming not merely that A_1 vastly exceeds A_2, but that B_1 somewhat exceeds B_2. If he accepts that argument then (if we ignore for a moment the alternative (C), however low he estimates $P(A)$ and however high he estimates $P(B)$), the rational man will become Christian. The improbability of the truth of the Christian theological system would be quite irrelevant, for the rewards of being Christian exceed the rewards of not being Christian whether or not the Christian theological system is true. This result could be upset by taking alternative C into account, only if – given an after-life but no Christian God – the evidence was that the Christian was less likely to have a happy after-life than was the non-Christian. But, if we ignore this possibility, then, if the preacher can convince men that B_1 exceeds

B_2, probabilities are irrelevant and the rational man will straightway become Christian. The humanist is of course perfectly entitled to counter these arguments by pointing out how even Heaven might pall (viz, that A_1 is not very large after all) and by describing the pleasure of his own worldly society.

The second feature of Christian apologetic on which our account sheds light is this. In so far as Christians have attempted to show the truth of their system, they have often been very much concerned to show how much more likely it is to be true than any other religious system, but not so concerned to show that it is more likely to be true than any non-religious system. My analysis brings out why this is so. Non-religious systems limit the duration of human life to life in this world, and hence the gains and losses of following any religious or non-religious policy are, if a non-religious system be true, very small compared with the gains and losses if the Christian system be true. Hence a non-religious system would have to be very much more probable than the Christian system for it to be rational to adopt it. Whereas rival religious systems offer their own eternal rewards and penalties and so, if their probability is anywhere near that of the Christian system, it will be in no way clear which it is rational to adopt. Hence it is important to the Christian preacher to show that their probability is not in that region. If $P(C)$ exceeds $P(A)$ and C_2 considerably exceeds C_1, then the policy of becoming a Christian may be the irrational policy – even if the joys of Christian life in the present exceed the joys of non-Christian life. For $P(A) = 0.05$, $P(B) = 0.85$, $P(C) = 0.1$, $A_1 = +1$, $A_2 = -1$, $B_1 = B_2$, $C_1 = -0.6$, $C_2 = +0.6$, the non-Christian policy will be the rational one. Now, true, in fact $P(C)$ covers many alternatives, on only some of which will the Christian be less well rewarded than the non-Christian, but these alternatives together must be shown to have a low probability, since the rewards and punishments will have a high positive or negative value in the regions respectively of A_1 and A_2. For this reason the Christian must show that Muhammad is no true prophet, and the Book of Mormon no true gospel. From earliest times Christians have been very much concerned to substantiate this kind of claim.

Yet, of course, there is more to religion than prudence. Moral considerations enter into our picture in two crucial ways. First the goals which we ought to seek are not merely those which we judge to be to our long-term advantage, not what we want, but what we ought to want for ourselves as well as for others. The preacher preaching the relative merits of the different systems tells men not merely that they will enjoy, say, Heaven but that life there will alone have meaning and purpose and that it it man's duty to seek such an existence for himself. But introducing morality into the ends does not disturb our calculus. We can use the same calculus to calculate the morally good as to calculate the long-term advantage. Yet although introducing morality into the ends may not upset the form of the calculus, it may make quite a difference to its matter. If we are concerned only with selfish advantage, there may well be some gain in living the non-Christian life. But the preacher may be able to persuade us that there is no moral good in it, and that the only life worth living is the life of Christian service here and hereafter. In that case we would hold that, however small the probability that the Christian theological system is true, we ought to become Christian. On the other hand the humanist preacher may be able to convince us that the Christian ideal of preserving oneself for a life hereafter, albeit a life of service, is not a worthy one. In that case we would hold that, whatever the possible selfish gain from doing so, we ought not to become Christian. Yet, if on the contrary, the evidence shows that the Christian system is probably true, then it shows that all deductive consequences of that system are probably true. One of these is that it is the duty of men to become Christian. However, considerations so far adduced suggest that it could be our duty to become Christian, even when the evidence suggests that the Christian theological system is probably false.

The other moral consideration which enters into our picture is perhaps the most crucial. It is this. We have seen that the Christian is one who believes certain propositions and lives out a certain kind of life. To decide to become a Christian involves – if we do not already believe them – deciding to take steps which would result in believing certain propositions. But even if a man can choose to believe, ought he to do so? Many would consider that it is highly immoral to choose to believe propositions (viz. to regard the evidence as supporting those propositions) when the evidence is now known not to support them. It would seem like lying to oneself. Others may be concerned with the fact that unless one is prepared to sacrifice one's beliefs in the service of the good, one is only half-committed to its pursuit. I do not wish to consider this moral issue in detail, but only to point out the consequences of different views about it. If a man claimed that there was nothing immoral in inducing in oneself any beliefs at all, not supported by present evidence,[11] then the position is as I have so far outlined it in this paper. The joys of Heaven (or the moral desirability of attempting to obtain them) and the horrors of Hell (or the moral wickedness of allowing oneself to risk obtaining them) provide reasons for inducing oneself to believe what seems on the evidence improbable. Many however would consider it morally wrong to induce oneself to believe what seems improbable. Yet these might hold a weaker position, that there is nothing immoral in choosing to believe one of two exhaustive alternatives between which we cannot decide by rational assessment of the evidence. By this I do not mean choosing to believe something with – by agreed standards of estimating probability – a probability of half; but choosing to believe something with – by one method of estimating probability – a probability of more than half, and – by another method of estimating – a probability of less than half, when it seems equally legitimate to use either method of estimating probability.

There are certain paradigm cases of events having on certain evidence certain numerical probabilities, and of events and theories being on certain evidence more probable than other events and theories. It is clear what is the probability relative to certain evidence of throwing two heads in a row or three sixes with three dice. But it is not always clear how we are to extrapolate standards of estimating probability from such simple cases to more complicated ones and on one way, one method of estimating probability, some theory T may have a probability of more than half, and on another way less than half. Yet both methods may appear equally natural ways of extrapolating from the paradigm cases. What ought one to do here? On one view one ought to average out the results given by the different methods. But there may be many methods, and the average results for the probability of theories and events from all methods may be all too often near to half. To average the results yielded by all possible methods might seem no less arbitrary than to decide to adopt one method of estimating probability, and thereby reach definite conclusions on matters previously unsettled. Such a decision would not be a decision to go against the evidence, but, at most, a decision to go beyond it. Yet such a decision would lead one to adopt beliefs previously not held. A man who felt it immoral to induce in himself beliefs not warranted by the evidence might well not feel it immoral to adopt one method of estimating probability rather than another, and this on grounds of which beliefs it would lead him to adopt.

Now the position in metaphysics may well be that there are various methods of estimating the probability of metaphysical theories and they are equally natural extrapolations from paradigm cases of ascribing probability to events and simpler theories. On one natural way of extrapolating from paradigm cases the evidence may indicate that the Christian theological system is probably true and on another way the evidence may indicate that the system is probably false; yet there be no rational grounds for choosing between the ways of assessing probability obtained by extrapolation from paradigm cases. In such circumstances a man might hold that it was not immoral to choose a method of estimating probability. Hence, he would hold, it would not be immoral to choose a method which led to certain assessments of probability rather than others.

Let us see in detail how, given that a man is allowed to choose between two different methods of estimating probability α and β, but not to choose to believe anything shown by both methods to have a probability of less than a half, he will work out the rational religious policy. Let us denote by $P_\alpha(A)$ the probability that state of affairs A holds on the method α of estimating probability, and so on. Let $P_\alpha(A)$ = 0.55, $P_\alpha(B)$ = 0.35, $P_\alpha(C)$ = 0.1, $P\beta(A)$ = 0.45; $P\beta(B)$ = 0.45, $P\beta(C)$ = 0.1. Let the man's estimates of the values of the outcomes be as follows:

$A_1 = 1$	$B_1 = -0.05$	$+1 \leqslant C_1 \leqslant -1$
$A_2 = -1$	$B_2 = +0.05$	$+1 \leqslant C_2 \leqslant -1$

Then on method α the expected gain of policy 1 will lie between 0.6325 and 0.4325 and of policy 2 between -0.4325 and -0.6325. On method β the expected gain of policy 1 will lie between 0.5275 and 0.3275, and of policy 2 between -0.3275 and -0.5275. Thus, whichever method of estimating probability be used, the expected gain of policy 1 will far outweigh the expected gain of policy 2. Hence if it is not immoral on other grounds to adopt it policy 1 ought to be adopted on these grounds. It will be immoral on other grounds only if thereby we decide to believe something shown to have a probability of less than a half by all legitimate methods of estimating probability. We do not do so in this case. We are deciding to believe something which, if we adopt a certain legitimate method of estimating probability, will have a probability of more than a half. It will therefore be rational to adopt that method of estimating probability. The numerical example which I chose is in one respect a simple one since the expected gain of one policy is greater than that of the other on both methods of estimating probability. It would be easy enough to devise an example in which the most rational policy will vary with the method of estimating probability which we adopt for calculating expected gain. In that case the pursuit of either policy would seem equally rational.

A man might however consider that the results of different methods of estimating probability ought always to be averaged arithmetically, in which case there will effectively be one resultant method of estimating probability; and that it is only legitimate to believe some system to be true if on that method the evidence now shows it to be probably true. In this case the rational man will become a Christian only if he judges that the evidence indicates that the Christian religion is probably true. He will not however necessarily become Christian even in that case, if we understand by the rational man the prudent man, for he may value so lowly the lives promised by the Christian theological system that the expected gain of becoming a Christian is outweighed by the gain of not becoming a Christian. Even if he judges that $P(A) > \frac{1}{2}$, B_2 may have such a high value in a man's estimation, that policy (2) is for him the most rational policy – so long as by 'rational' policy is meant prudential policy. Yet if a man held that $P(A) > \frac{1}{2}$, he would hold that the consequences of the Christian system were probably true and these include the consequence that all men ought to become Christians. In that case if the rational man is the man who pursues the morally right policy, he would become a Christian.

My problem was whether it was a necessary and sufficient condition for the rational man becoming a Christian that he judges that the evidence available to him shows that the probability that the Christian theological system is true is greater than a half. My conclusion is that it depends on how one interprets 'rational' and what are one's views about the morality of believing what is probably false. I have illustrated in detail how these considerations affect the issue, and how on some views on the moral issue the cited condition is not a necessary condition, and how on a non-moral understanding of 'rational' it is not a sufficient condition, for the rational man to become a Christian.

NOTES

1. I am most grateful to G. Wallace and C. J. F. Williams for their helpful criticisms of an earlier version of this paper.
2. H. H. Price, 'Belief "In" and Belief "That" ', *Religious Studies*, 1965, Vol. 1, pp. 5-27.
3. B. Pascal, *Pensées,* No. 233.
4. *Ibid., loc. cit.*
5. *Ibid.,* No. 195.
6. B. Pascal, *Pensées,* No. 233.
7. This point has been well made by (e.g.) Anthony Flew. See his *God and Philosophy* (London, 1966), 9.9 *et seq.*
8. David Hume, *A Treatise of Human Nature,* Appendix, p. 624 in the edition edited by L. A. Selby-Bigge (Oxford, 1888).
9. See H. H. Price, 'Belief and Will', *Proceedings of the Aristotelian Society Supplementary Volume,* 1954, 28, pp. 1-26, who develops this point at length.
10. *Ibid.,* No. 233.
11. Price adopts this view in the paper referred to above at note 9.

QUESTIONS for further discussion:

Are there no considerations which might properly dispose a rational policy adopter to foster in himself religious *un*belief? As Pascal and Swinburne survey alternative policies for living there are some contentions, even some drawn from standard Christian teaching, to which they do not devote attention but which may reasonably prompt the prudent person to cultivate unbelief rather than belief.

Christian tradition (see Luke 12, 47-8; 23, 34) and perhaps most people's moral leanings, suggest that the *believer* who fails to live up to the standards set by his faith, fails to live out his life in anything like the appropriate style will be and should be more severely judged than the unbeliever who behaves similarly but in some respects does not know (if Christianity is true) what he is doing.

Again, there is some suggestion in Christian tradition (e.g. John 3, 19) that the wicked person is under particular condemnation in so far as he has been confronted by and has rejected the light and truth which (?who) is Christ; and this seems to have the corollary that it would have been better for him if such a person had not been thus confronted. It may be better therefore for the modern wicked man if he does not apprehend Jesus Christ as Christians claim Him to be, or indeed at all.

Paper VIII
Introductory Groundwork

For most people, whether they are believers or not, the world's evils constitute the most obvious and commonly pressed difficulty for reasonable belief in God. If God is almighty and loving to the utmost, then, it has seemed, He has both the power and the will to eliminate at least some of what we regard as pointless, unnecessary, unjust, immense evil which is present in the world. Either He does not regard it as evil, (in which case His goodness (and perhaps His omniscience) is called in question), or He cannot exclude such evils from this world, (in which case His almightiness is in question), or He does not will to exclude what He does regard as evil (in which case His love is in question). Rational belief, it seems, requires that an account be constructed of the cosmic situation in which the existence of God (good, almighty, all-loving, as He is conceived of in the Judaeo–Christian tradition) is *at the least* not incompatible with the facts, including the facts about evil, of the world. Minimally, then this account may be offered only as a *possibility*, showing that, at any rate, the facts about the evils in the world are not logically incompatible with the existence of God. The account *may* claim more in claiming to say not only how things may possibly be, but also how things actually are, setting out to justify the ways of God to man.

Clark's paper only briefly attends to this sort of standard theodicy. (For further treatment see e.g. J. Hick, *Evil and the God of Love*, 1965, or A. Plantinga, *God, Freedom and Evil*, 1975.) He leaves the way open to a possible theodicy when he says '. . . the Creator was under no obligation to destroy the world He got when He created, only to create as good a world as He could. There then arises the question whether even the Omniscient can know the quality of merely imaginary worlds: perhaps He must create in order to know what the world He creates is like, and having created should sustain it till it can achieve its own felicity.' However, for the most part here Clark is interested in pursuing questions which must still be raised even if that sort of theodicy fails. For example the difficulty, or persons who pose the difficulty as their own, must presuppose that human evaluative judgments as to what is good or evil are not merely expressions of likes and preferences which an individual or a group happens to have, but are judgments which *justify* rejecting theism, judgments with which, probably, all should concur. But has a person the right to claim this for his evaluations if these evaluations are the product of a universe whose people are neither created nor enlightened by a good God, a divine, good, Spirit? (A similar issue arises for any of our claims to recognise *truth*, if our cognitive faculties are the products of a universe neither ordered nor inspired by the divine.) If not, then what is judged to be evil in the world is a problem for theism, if and only if theism of some sort is supposed; modern atheistic rational humanism, (in Clark's view typically, but in view of its own theoretical undermining of any human moral seriousness, perhaps unsurprisingly responsible for much it deplores in God), is mere superstition in affirming and trusting a morality whose existence it cannot justifiably claim. In what follows Diabolus is spokesman for this rational humanism.

Theism of a standard Judaeo–Christian or Islamic sort is not the only alternative to the rejected contentions of Diabolus. Ancient Gnosticism in most of its varied forms distinguished between on the one hand the creator and controller of the experienced world in time and space, the physical world, who is evil, from whose evil world we need deliverance (in Clark's paper bearing the name 'Ialdobaoth') and the Good God, or Great First Light by whose enlightenment deliverance is possible. If such enlightenment can be conceived of as taking place independently of processes of, or events in, the material world, Gnostic doctrine may offer an advance on mainstream theism, but if our mental life is correlated with (some parts of) the physical world, mainstream theism is, rather, preferable. As a further possibility we may choose to try to forget the pains of this world and to secure for ourselves what unquestioning anxiety-free comfort we can.

As he discusses these options Clark touches on a number of important long debated topics, as: whether what God commands is good because God commands it or He commands it because, apart from His commands, it is good (the *Euthyphro* dilemma, from Plato's dialogue of that name); whether beings such as Googols or mad scientists (p. 127) may, unknown to us, affect our cognitive processes, as Descartes supposed a demon may do. The choice, between Theism, or Gnosticism, on the one hand, and on the other comfortable selective attention and cultivated forgetfulness, is a choice which reason does not determine, since, in Clark's view, to trust reason and suppose it to lead us to the truth and to make correct evaluations is effectively to have decided for the former. There is point therefore, in describing this paper as setting before us the nature and implications of our choice of *faith* (and one might add hope and love) or our rejection of it.

God, Good and Evil

STEPHEN R. L. CLARK

My topics are the problem of evil and the supposed autonomy of ethics.[1] I wish to suggest that the discussion of these problems has often been vitiated by taking them separately, and that the former problem has at least as destructive an effect on rational humanism as it does on theism. I shall make use of Gnostic speculations, and of the Valentinian name for the world-archon, Ialdobaoth. I shall refer to my opponent, my *alter ego*, as Diabolus.

The phenomenal universe appears to contain physical and moral evils that would be signs of cruelty and injustice if they were laid to the charge of a will competent to avoid them. Efforts to mitigate these horrors, as being necessary but minor evils leading to, or consequent upon the possibility of, a supremely worthwhile state of being, rarely convince Diabolus. Perhaps a finite power could be excused for its hamfistedness or for the regrettable by-products of its well-meaning industry. An infinitely capable power, who has selected his own parameters, his own causal laws, his tools, his very ends, can hardly escape judgment by such appeals to 'happenstance', *force majeure* and ignorance. The phenomenal universe is not the sort of thing we would whole-heartedly compliment any Cosmic Engineer for having produced. To be sure: since that Engineer (if he exists at all) has cunningly endowed us with an unreasoning pleasure in our continued existence (thereby multiplying misery), we may be inclined to think that such existence defies gratitude. Any existence is so infinitely superior to non-entity that its Creator owes us nothing more. That may be the final and only answer to our complaints, that the potter does not argue with the pot. What we are, He made us, and our very complaints are by His courtesy. 'For without Him who can enjoy his food, or who be anxious?' (*Ecclesiastes* 2.25 (N.E.B.)). But such resignation does not come by argument. Surely, Diabolus insists, a woman who knowingly conceived a child destined for physical deformity, social ostracism, moral corruption would still be at fault even though that child itself has not been *wronged*? She has freely increased the sum of misery. What is the point of saying that she should not act so if the God of all gods Himself does it and is praised for doing so? Perhaps all creation involves risks (though the Omnicompetent should surely avoid most of them) and perhaps creation is nonetheless a 'good thing', but there are degrees beyond which the wilful creation of suffering, whatever its attendant goods or opposing virtues, is simply incompatible with any will that we should normally praise. Moral goods, such as courage in the face of evil or forgiveness for the sin of cruelty, may require that there be evil (both physical and moral), but it is not clear that such virtues are more than *pis-allers*. As Aristotle remarked (*Nicomachean Ethics* X.1178b1of), we cannot properly attribute them to gods in a divine universe. Nor do we praise men who torment their children to cultivate their moral character, even if their predictions are correct (though in this we perhaps differ from our forefathers). Consider also William Blake's acid jest: 'Pity would be no more if we did not make somebody poor' (*Songs of Experience*). And again: It is not wholly certain that the Omnicompetent could not cause there to be (what are clearly logical possibilities) beings who freely and invariably choose the right, despite temptations to err. It is admittedly also not certain that He could, for if we take time seriously at all even God can only create free beings who are *likely* not to sin: beings who are certain never to sin cannot be considered free agents. But in other contexts than the problem of free will theists have been less eager to claim clear knowledge of what self-contradiction is in the case of deity. All these traditional moves in the game are profoundly unconvincing to Diabolus.

My strategy is to accept the charge: the phenomenal universe is not such as we can easily imagine a decent creator's creating or sustaining. Any will that willed or was willing to accept the biosphere's multiple ingenuities of torture, or permitted the corruption and suffering of tyranny's victims in all ages, is not a will that we should normally consider good. If the Galactic Empire has observers on the Earth they are absolved of criminal responsibility only in so far as they are themselves subject to laws and generalities not of their own making. The God of religion, of course, is experienced in cult and meditation as being confronted by us as problems which He must solve under the rubric of general laws: as such He is presumably excusable. But it is an article of faith that He has posed Himself the problem, and Himself decrees those laws: the excuse wears rather thin.

Very well: the phenomenal universe is not worth sustaining. The attempt to argue otherwise is reminiscent of traditional anthropodicies: 'There is much talk of the misery which we cause to the brute creation; but they are recompensed by existence. If they were not useful to man, and therefore protected by him, they would not be nearly so numerous' (Samuel Johnson: *Boswell's Life*, May 1776, p. 753). But as Boswell commented, there is a question whether the animals would accept existence on their present terms. If it is wrong for the Omni-competent to sustain the world in misery, it is surely wrong for us to excuse ourselves by arguments which are that much less plausible by how much our powers are less (for it is not entirely true that our victims owe their lives to us, save in the sense that we have not yet taken them).[2]

This point has a very general significance: if the world is not such as can be decently sustained by one who has the power to do other-wise, then we cannot decently sustain it either. We cannot decently continue to cooperate in phenomenal existence. We ought to preach sterility, and seek ways of eliminating all conscious or sentient being. Professional philosophers, of course, have made their own compro-mises with the powers-that-be: their pupils may one day astonish us. The Gnostic philosophers were more consistent in their hostility. Only a savage, or at best a power just without mercy, could have made the world, and in denouncing that Creator they abjured his work. Copu-lation was evil just in that it was procreative, and their enemies accused them of promiscuity, *coitus interruptus*, abortion and the ceremonial eating of embryos. Gnostics (and Buddhists, who have a similarly low opinion of Brahma) are indeed less committed to a policy of genocide than Diabolus. For they suppose the world to be fundamentally mentalistic: material suicide will not release us from the Wheel – for that, if it is possible at all, a lengthier discipline is necessary. A ma-terialistic Diabolus has an easy solution for his *ennui*. To be sure: even the Last War can only purge the Earth, and there may be millions of inhabited worlds still under the yoke. But if the undefined weight of those millions is to weaken our resolve to eliminate what evil we can it must cast all our projects into doubt. If it is not worth the bother of genocide, it is not worth the bother of continued living, for nothing we can do (on these terms) makes more than an infinitesimal difference.

Diabolus has a reply. The world is not such as can decently be sustained by one who can do better (as the Omnicompetent could). But we do not better the world by destroying it, or the awareness of it. The world is made of grain and chaff obscurely mixed: we have a duty to improve it, or at least not to make it worse. We do not have a duty to destroy it. By the same token, of course, the Creator was under no obligation to destroy the world He got when He created, only to create as good a world as He could. There then arises the question whether even the Omniscient can know the quality of merely imaginary worlds: perhaps He must create in order to know what the world He creates is like, and having created should sustain it till it can achieve its own felicity. I have no answer to this question, and will continue to accept that the world is not one that a decent Creator can easily be supposed to have created. Diabolus, at any rate, is (so far) permitted to live. But of course he is permitted to live only at the price of making the world better, or not making it worse. The Karamazovs agreed that they would not purchase universal felicity by torturing a baby to death (*Brothers Karamazov* V.4) – and doubtless they did well in this, for there is only one salesman who would offer such a bargain, and he is not noted for his fidelity. But our agents and our moralists regularly defend the torture of innocents for the sake of goods much less enticing than universal felicity. Flesh-foods, cosmetics, aspirins and indigestion tablets to alleviate the effects of nicotine-poisoning or over-eating are all purchased at the price of extreme suffering and deprivation on the part of our non-human cousins. If Ialdobaoth is condemned, like Soame Jenyns' celestial *voyeurs*, so also are we.[3] All spokesmen for Diabolus, and particularly those who make much of animal suffering, should seek to separate themselves from our millenial tyranny, so as not to make the world worse than they have to, and so as not to be like the God they hate. Gnostics and Buddhists often do so: I had not observed that modern spokesmen for Diabolus were so honourable. In condemning Ialdobaoth we condemn ourselves.

Diabolus may reply that his attack upon the Creator is, as it were, *ad hominem*. It is not that he disapproves, nor commits himself to avoidance of the moral evil he condemns, but merely that he denies such a being any title to the justice and compassion predicated of Him in the theistic tradition. But this response is clearly not in full accord with the moral seriousness of his original charge, and allows the apologist to evade the real point: that only the 'good' are worthy of worship.

Diabolus may also insist that his charge against Ialdobaoth is that He has occasioned animal suffering that is unnecessary to human welfare or even wholly unhelpful. Diabolus is therefore licensed to torture to obtain human advantage even while attacking Ialdobaoth for using torture for His own purposes. The fact remains that we too cause unnecessary suffering, even if Ialdobaoth could avoid more than we. Nor can I see why Ialdobaoth is not allowed to torture for His purposes if we are allowed to torture for ours. At the very least a Gestapo officer is in no very strong position to condemn Ialdobaoth, and neither is the rational humanist, unless he changes his ways.

Again, Diabolus may remark that it is not obviously true that just the same behaviour is required of a 'good pantocrator' and a good man, any more than identically the same behaviour (except under the general description of 'doing the right thing') is required of good young men and good old women. This is not to accept an account of theological language as uniquely analogical: simply to remember that 'good' is not straightforwardly descriptive. It does not follow that because good men work to support their families good children must do likewise: our duties may be more specialised than that, and what is required of pantocrators may not be required of us. But of course, if Diabolus does insist on this, he leaves himself open to the reply that the duties of pantocrators cannot so easily be deduced from the duties of men. Despite Descartes, we cannot properly conclude that a good pantocrator would not deceive us, nor that He would not hurt us. He may do both if He conceives it to be for the final good of His creatures and Himself, and there is no speedier, less hurtful way: and of that we cannot be certain.

Diabolus would be better advised to stick to Mill's challenge: 'I will call no being good, who is not what I mean when I apply that epithet to my fellow creatures; and if such a being can sentence me to hell for not so calling him, to hell I will go' (Nelson Pike (ed.) *God and Evil* p. 43). Mill's own criteria for goodness, of course, render it difficult to force the case against Ialdobaoth: utilitarian considerations and a respect for individual liberty may compel Ialdobaoth to allow passing evils. God can operate a utilitarian ethic too: indeed, it seems likely that only the Omniscient and Omnicompetent could do so. If His utilitarianism is unbearable, our own clumsy calculus had better be abandoned too. But Mill's challenge still stands as an inspiring defiance of the powers-that-be, a defiance that moralising philosophers are inclined to consider heroic. It is a challenge, however, with some odd features. A psycho-analyst friend of mine, perhaps more aware of the treacheries of the human heart, once wrote to me that he *hoped*, if there turned out to be a God, that he would have the courage to spit, as it were, in His face. He *hoped*: it may be that he only meant that he would be glad if he did, or was glad to think that he would, or would be glad to be sure that he was going to – though none of these para-phrases quite catches what is meant by 'hoping'. We do not have to accept Marcel's judgment that 'hope is a desperate appeal to an ally who is Himself also Love' (*Being and Having* 17.3.1931) to agree that hope involves a partial conviction that something in the universe at least might be on one's side.[4] And if God is against us, who shall be for us? *'Who* durst defy th'Omnipotent to arms?' Or rather, who can? How exactly did Mill expect to defy that power which sustained his existence? To whom was my friend, half-consciously, appealing for help to stand firm? 'Pray God that I may be granted grace to defy God to the very end!' And perhaps he will.

This is to emphasise the point I have already mentioned, that our complaints are by His courtesy. There is a curious lack of fit between the content of Diabolus' accusation and its existence. At its crudest the charge is that God is responsible for all that goes on, but in making the charge Diabolus presents himself as an independent agent over against God. But either there are independent agents or there are not: if there are, then God is not responsible for the evil they do; if there are not then Diabolus deceives himself, and should recognise that his hope (?) of being Prometheus is simply another act of God. In less crude forms, avoiding the pragmatic inanity of determinism, Diabolus' complaints are rather that God allows to His independent creatures more liberty than Diabolus would wish. Diabolus wants to be allowed to complain: he does not want others to be allowed to do what they want to do. The classical fear was that God was a tyrant (but if He is, He is too successful for any extrinsic judgment); the more modern, liberal slander is that He is a do-nothing. In short, we now complain not that He performs judgment, but that He exercises mercy (or at least delay). 'O God, if only thou wouldst slay the wicked!' (*Psalm* 139.19): 'but He is very patient with you, for it is not His will for any to be lost, but for all to come to repentance' (*2 Peter* 3.9). Those who call for judgment may find at last that it comes.

To put the same point slightly differently: Diabolus may say that

God has indeed (by hypothesis) created us as independent agents, so that we may both accuse Him and ourselves work evil against His will. If we are so far independent of Him that we may sin, that is His fault, and we are entitled to say so. But the price of being able to complain is that we are also able to sin – that is, to take offence at the workings of God's providence. Would the world really be better if we disallowed such liberty?

A further oddity in Mill's defiance also harks back to an earlier point. When some sadistic moron shows a Jain extremist the manifold life he must destroy in drinking water, and that Jain at once defies the world to do its tawdry worst and forswears food and drink thereafter our hearts do not beat high. We can hardly restrain our scorn for such 'noble foolishness'. What good does it do? Sensible people 'accept the universe', and we murmur 'God, they'd better'. Even where unconventional conduct would cost us nothing, amateur and professional moralists constantly appeal to the fact that creatures commonly behave in a certain way to 'prove' that we can have no moral duty to behave otherwise. If fish eat fish we are entitled to copy their example, even while proclaiming our own superiority to such exemplars. We oddly denounce the hypothetical Creator and His works at the same time as assuming that the world enshrines an adequate standard for our own behaviour. But why? Why is it noble to defy God, but merely silly to adopt other standards than, let alone to defy, the world? A storm is no greater an evil for being caused by an evil spirit (S. Johnson: Boswell's *Journal of a tour to the Hebrides* 16th August), though this may add a further, moral evil. If we should disobey and despise the will that perhaps occasions storms, disease and corruption, we should surely (at the least) take some pains not to act like that ourselves, and even to reject all profit from cooperation in such a sinister universe. If Mill was ready to reject all future felicity when offered him by a Creator Devil, why should he accept is so readily at the world's hands? If on the contrary we should make the best we can of what is offered us, what offence is there in joining the only, and celestial, game in town? Or is the point simply and discreditably that we do not expect our bluff to be called? God is bound to prefer our noble outspokenness to the cowardice of sycophantic churchmen (though I cannot see why He should therefore give us credit for what is His gift to us), or at least our fellow-men will be more impressed by those who pretend to call the Omnicompetent to court.

Stephen R. L. Clark

But whose court? 'If only there were one to arbitrate between us' (*Job* 9.32). The Gnostic Adam took his lawsuit to the Great First Life (Mandaean GT 437: H. Jonas *The Gnostic Religion* p. 88), and it was by the standard of eternity that the archons were judged. It is because we are, or there is something more than the archons, that we have an escape. It is because there is an unborn, an indestructible, as Gautama taught, that there is an exit from the Wheel. If there is not, whose court is it we call to?

Diabolus at once replies that ethics are autonomous, that they owe nothing to the dictates of a celestial Augustus, that they are supremely super-empirical. The laws of justice are binding even if they are never operative; the innocent are in the right even if they are never vindicated. Diabolus, rather oddly, is sometimes even inclined to think that ethics, to avoid vulgarity, must be empirically unsuccessful, even while denouncing God and His creation for not vindicating the oppressed. It is wrong that justice does not prosper, but it would also be wrong if it did. More circumspectly, Diabolus insists that there need be no actual court of appeal, no power in the world, that could successfully condemn Ialdobaoth; yet nonetheless Ialdobaoth is condemned *morally* in the hearts of all honourable men by the independent standards of right and wrong. That he cannot be brought to trial in the outer world is unfortunate, but at least we know what verdict would be given.

Philosophers have disagreed about the nature of these intuited standards. It is perhaps significant for my thesis that Platonism, one of the most determined attempts to depict them as eternal realities independent of phenomena and of the observing mind, was historically unstable: the Ideas ended up as the thoughts of God. It is, however, possible that some sort of Platonism could cope with the problems I shall raise. My principal quarrel, though, is with such modern spokesmen for Diabolus as are unlikely to appeal to such objective Ideas. Indeed, even if they did I suspect that my point would apply. For whatever the truth about objective morality our experience or intuition of morality is a matter of our own deep-seated preferences, antipathies, reasonings and feelings or respect. These either are themselves the content of ethics or our route to the ethical.

Even the Creator then must be judged by the deep-seated impulses and careful reasonings that He has implanted in us. We need no further court. But it is surely obvious that in condemning Him we cast doubt on our own ethical intuitions, unless these are held to come from Outside. The first move of any coherent Gnosticism is to adopt an ascetic renunciation of the desires of the flesh; the second is to brand the ethical law, in the Torah or in our own heart, as a further device of tyranny. The ascetic and antinomian modes of Gnosticism may alternate or even be conjoined in a sort of professional sado-masochism that practises, for example, promiscuity precisely insofar as it can be made repellent. A third move, of course, would be to reject even the reasonings that led to this or any other conclusion, and so to stand naked in the Void. If the Creator is evil (what we call 'evil'), and there is no escape from His world, or at any rate no clear signpost to the exit, then as we cannot even count upon His keeping His threats and promises (C. S. Lewis *A Grief Observed* p. 28) we no longer have any idea what to do for the best or what that best might be. Neither have we any coherent ground for thinking the Creator evil. That way lies madness.

My point is not a parochial one. Gnostics spoke of Ialdobaoth, but their systems could with equal cogency be outlined in purely materialistic terms. This universe of unpurposed force, greed, self-centredness and pain has accidently produced in the last few thousand years a species and a culture which professes, though it does not act upon, a liking for justice, compassion, logical rigour and so forth. Materialistic accounts of evolution have begun, though only begun, to devise detailed explanations for our having such preferences, both the ones that we share with all mammals or all primates and those that are peculiar to our species or culture. Of course the mere fact that there are such physical or sociological explanations for our thinking and feeling as we do does not of itself disprove or disallow those thoughts and feelings (though Diabolus sometimes assumes otherwise when dealing with religion). If evolutionary logic has produced beings who believe theses *p, q, r,* those very theses may still be true. But if evolutionary logic is a full explanation for our belief it is at least unnecessary to suppose our belief veridical unless we can independently show it to be true. But it can be shown to be true only, for us, by being shown to be evident (*i.e.,* believed) or to be logically dependent upon some other, evident belief. And the concept of logical dependency, as well as the variety of immediate beliefs have, by hypothesis, been generated in us (or we have been generated having them) through physical processes that have no relevance nor reference to the truth or metaphysical necessity of those concepts and beliefs. Our beliefs may be true, but we have no warrant for believing them: indeed we can no longer have any confidence in the notion of having or needing a ground for belief. From which it follows, if anything now does, that the whole materialistic account of our history becomes, not obviously false, but simply unauthorised.

The situation might be saved by claiming that our beliefs and our belief-forming systems have been selected for and reinforced by past success, so that we have at least this much reason to think them true, or at least to think materialism coherent. I doubt if this works, both because of usual problems about inductive inference and because the story of our past evolutionary success is itself on trial, but I am willing to allow that our cognitive situation may not be beyond repair. But our affective, and therefore our ethical, responses are critically affected by Diabolus' system. When we come to believe of ourselves that we have certain affective preferences only because of childhood indoctrination or genetic determinism we may continue to feel those preferences, but we are almost bound to take them less seriously. We feel no compunction, and perhaps some enthusiasm, at educating ourselves out of them, and take no trouble to impose them on others, save to the limited extent that by doing so we facilitate our own satisfactions. So far my point is perhaps rather laboured: certainly the Laodicean tolerance currently popular, as well as that inane morality that denounces those who seek to persuade others to their own moral convictions, suggests that many people have digested the implications of Diabolus' creed. Morality, considered as binding upon oneself and others, is confusedly considered illiberal. The confusion should grow. For we are continuing to assess our moral preferences, or what were once moral preferences, in terms of other preferences which we have allowed to stand, such as a wish for security, for human solidarity, for the survival of oneself and one's kind, for pleasure. But Diabolus' critique has put other names on these passions: cowardice, racism, greed. Pleasure is the bait in the scented trap of procreation, kinship the outward sign of neo-Darwinian competition. In showing the world to be depraved by the very standards we have come to have, and in showing, admittedly rather sketchily, that our standards are accidental products of just those depraved processes, he has cast doubt on our most basic preferences.There is no reason to think that acting on them leads to anything we might reasonably call good;

there is no reason to take seriously our attitudes of respect, obedience, affection. It is not even that we are not *bound* to follow them, but may: rather, if we do follow them we are bound to consider the process of their begetting to be untrustworthy, or despicable. Morality is a superstition that has revealed its foundations to be quintessentially immoral. To love men is to hate the non-human; to seek pleasure is to propagate pain; to respect authority is to acquiesce in evil. It is not surprising that an uneasy relativism in ethics is often conjoined with a naive worship of natural processes: the same man may jeer at those who take morality so seriously as to act upon it to their own disadvantage and himself read moral lessons from the fact that creatures generally do behave in some way – 'whatever is, is right', but without Pope's reason. This is not surprising: if we cannot force ourselves to believe that what happens is good we must be alienated from our own inclinations, unless we can invoke some transcendental standard and origin for our moral inclinations. How otherwise, in particular, can we take seriously the species-centred conceit that has begotten humanism? Men are my kind of creature? But this is to say only that our ancestors had certain preferences and antipathies: inter-racial antagonisms may yet produce a number of hominid species – will members of one such species then be licensed to do as they please to members of another, just because their ancestors did? Those who think so are in no position to denounce Ialdobaoth, lest they thereby both condemn themselves and destroy the moral standing of their creed.

Diabolus may retort, once more, that his claim is only that the universe is such that its hypothetical Creator must have very different priorities and purposes from those which we associate with the good. 'My ways are not your ways, says the Lord' (*Isaiah* 55.8), and Diabolus sardonically agrees. But this response misses his own moral seriousness in the charge and leaves it unclear why the theist must be puzzled. Plainly the pantocrator does not consider Himself bound by all the laws He proclaims to us: '*Thou* shalt not kill', but God reserves that privilege to Himself. 'Vengeance is mine, says the Lord' (*Romans* 12.19). There are things that God does not allow us to do: it is hardly a surprise to find that He gives Himself more latitude. Certainly we cannot discover what we may do from an enquiry into what naturally happens, even if that is by God's providence. That there are miscarriages in pregnancy no more licenses embryonicide than murder is licensed by the fact of natural death.

On the other hand, 'You shall be holy, for I the Lord your God am holy' (*Leviticus* 19.2). And again: 'Be perfect, as your heavenly Father is perfect' (*Matthew* 5.48). We are commanded to be like Him, and if we are like Him we are being, and doing good. The problem of evil is precisely that not everything that naturally happens is the sort of thing that we could bring about and still hope to be called good. We are to be like God, but not always to act as He seems to. Some, but not all, natural processes are to be endorsed, and in endorsing them we accept God's judgment on ourselves and on the world. God's righteousness, *sedeq*, consists in the supreme consistency of His nature, and His consequent fidelity to the covenants formed between Himself and His creation (J. Pedersen, *Israel I-II* pp. 338f). These covenants require of us a perpetual remembrance that the world does not belong to us, and compassion particularly for the weak and defenceless: 'rights' operate chiefly to protect those who are unable to negotiate contracts by their own power.

How are these points to be related to standard philosophical arguments, beginning from Plato's *Euthyphro*, for the autonomy of ethics? Must not even God's commands be obeyed only for non-moral reasons, out of fear or affection, unless they merely transmit moral obligation? To base one's conduct on messages from a celestial Augustus is surely to abandon morality. Such a god may, if he is of good character and sound moral judgment, command what is right, but it would still be right even if he commanded the opposite, and to do what he says only because he says it is to display moral myopia. Perhaps he may change his mind? Surely, to say that he is good must be more than to say he is self-consistent?

Such arguments are often repeated without due attention. It is worth asking Diabolus what reason he can imagine himself giving for saying that something commanded by God is in fact 'wrong'. 'God tells us to love our enemies, but I think He's quite wrong.' One who has invented all the things that His creatures enjoy, and determines the causal laws that lead to enjoyment or its opposite, presumably gives better advice than Diabolus. Again, what good could we ever do by disobeying the Omnipotent? The good of not consenting to iniquity, perhaps (although the evil thing will still be done), but I have already pointed to our strange unwillingness to avoid such a consent in the case of natural event. And in any case, if a command is seriously experienced as iniquitous it cannot simultaneously be attributed to God,

124

not because God is bound to obey an independent moral code, but because our perception of God's commands is precisely mediated in our serious moral convictions. Nor is it sensible to speak of 'God's changing His mind', as if He were a creature subject to inconsistencies of judgment, mood and temper. It may be absurd to suppose that rape might be a moral duty; it is just as absurd to imagine God's suddenly commanding it, and hardly surprising that one absurdity follows from another. What of Abraham and Isaac? Well, what of them? Abraham did not kill his son, but he incurred no moral guilt at all by seeking to do so (how else should he save his son alive?), nor can any intelligible charge be made out against the Creator either for threatening Isaac's life or requiring Abraham to be His agent. Or if one can, it presumably also stands against all moral systems that require that personal or parental ties be subordinated to civic or universal justice.

Diabolus may be induced to agree that those acts commanded by God and those acts that are morally obligatory both are and must be identical, but he will still insist that these properties are distinct. If an act is right we have a reason to perform it which is quite independent of God's demanding it. Theistic moralists lend support to this point by claiming that their own particular version of God's commandments is the sole route to personal and social welfare. If it is, then it would be good even if *per impossibile* God did not demand it, and it remains good even if God does not exist at all.

It is not in fact obvious to me that anything can be morally good or obligatory in the absence of God. We can imagine that we might desire things even in a godless universe (though the careful imagination of such a universe must surely tend to make us think our desires futile), but such good (i.e., desired) things might not then be in any sense morally good, such as should be required of all moral agents. It seems not unlikely to me that moral obligations are literally owed to someone or to Someone, just as legal obligations are. If philosophers can interpret the rules of justice as those which ignorant participants-to-be would accept, I do not think it impossible that moral laws should similarly be interpreted as those dictates which an omniscient and impartially benevolent judge would deliver, if he existed. What motive we could have for doing what such a fiction suggests I do not know, and it should at least perturb Diabolus that if he accepts such an analysis as valid he comes close to acknowledging that God must at least be possible – and if possible, then necessary (by the Ontological

Argument in its valid second form).

But it is enough for my purposes to claim, not that being obligatory and being God's command are the very same thing (even if the atheist fails to draw the proper conclusion from his superstitious respect for moral obligation), but only that it is God who makes things to be obligatory, just as He makes things to be facts. For whenever Diabolus pretends to be judging God's commands and finding them (at best) in accordance with moral goodness, he forgets what was a major plank of his argument with respect to the problem of evil: namely, that it is the Creator who selects and sustains the causal laws governing or describing events. If justice, charity and compassion pay it is because He has decreed that they should. If they excite an immediate respect in us it is because He has made us so. Such reasonings are not, therefore, independent of God's will, but rather constitute (part of) the promulgation of that will. 'It is surely wicked deliberately to inflict pain unnecessarily because of the nature of pain, and not primarily because God decreed that it should be' (A. C. Ewing in I. Ramsey (ed.) *The Problem of Evil* p. 42). But by hypothesis it is God that envisaged our sense of physiological damage (which He also envisaged) as being *pain*, a thing that all with any will in the matter must in the first instance seek to escape. In creating it as such He has declared it an evil. Every other motive for being just, or suggested analysis of what it is to be good, depends upon God's creative activity, if He exists at all.

The atheist of course may experience moral demands upon him, though if I am right he is likely to take such natural impulses less and less seriously (and thereby lose any standing in the charge against Ialdobaoth). The theist cannot suppose that he has any independent, authoritative standards against which to judge God's judgments or His mighty acts. If he turns rebel, his 'heroic defiance' of the Creator come down at last to the self-alienating cry of 'Evil, be thou my good', the attempt to be as far as possible (i.e., as far as God allows) what oneself most hates. Only the most extreme of moralists(?) can really find this sort of sado-masochism attractive. Certainly Diabolus cannot, on these terms, make much of a case against Ialdobaoth.

The paradox to which I am pointing is just this: that only if we can conceive that some natural processes and impulses are divinely created, can we find any sure ground from which to pass judgment on other natural processes. If everything that happens is good, there is no charge against the Creator. But if everything that happens is bad, there can also be no charge against Him; nor yet can there be if everything happens merely by nature. An archon, such as Ialdobaoth, can be judged and condemned by the Standards of the Great First Life, sparks from which still inhabit his world. If, as seems likely, we cannot draw any clear line between the action of those sparks and the action of natural law, we must allow that there is a closer link between the Great First Life and the phenomenal world than the Gnostics thought. What we cannot do is to denounce the Creator and simultaneously deny the existence of a world independent of His. Nor, I think, can we maintain any conviction of moral seriousness if we allow the problem of evil to dissuade us from theism. Moral atheism, rational humanism are simply superstitions, and Diabolus, in raising the problem of evil against God, demonstrates only that his heart is more religious than his head.

My claim as a theist is that Goodness is God: that is, that there is an actual and not merely a possible satisfaction of all desire in the enjoyment of an eternal life that is both the final end and, beyond all expectation, the first cause of the phenomenal world. I have not sought to explain how, perhaps by our own hubristic or adventurous choice, the Great First Life is now so strangely manifested. My point has been that the problem of evil is not a problem only for theists, and is therefore no particular refutation of theism. My final point is concerned also with epistemology.

Marcion went further even than most Gnostics in declaring that nature was corrupt beyond redemption. For him all our nature is of the Dark, and the transcendent Light has revealed itself at one point only in all cosmic history, in the teaching of the Lord Jesus Christ. The God and Father of Jesus is utterly alien to our nature, and to the world we inhabit. Action in accord with His commands can earn us no temporal advantage nor psychological assurance. Here even more than in other Gnostic systems pragmatic success and truth are fiercely divided. The Marcionite is in the same case as victims of Lehrer's Googols or Unger's mad scientist: for all 'practical' purposes he inhabits a phenomenal world that is wholly spurious, and truth is wholly metaphysical. As far as experience goes, his 'truth' is a fantasy realm in which he can evade the pressing claims of ordinary 'reality'. The standard answers to sceptical arguments are implicitly Pyrrhonian, not to say Pyrrhic, to the effect that we need only consider the consistency of phenomena, need not answer transcendental questions about the epistemological status of our experience, have no apparent hope of discerning the 'truth' and therefore no need of such a category. Maybe the 'truth' was shown, by the Googols' carelessness, to a solitary and seeming lunatic, but that sort of truth is useless to us. What matters is that we should live agreeably with our friends, or those we find it agreeable to suppose friends, in ready ignorance of transcendental doubt. Even that ghostly counterpart of the phenomenal world, namely the material universe, should not be taken too seriously: we can only think our concerns important if we forget the physical conditioning that makes us take them so and the enormities of time and space that dwarf any serious utilitarian concern. If we are truly limited to non-transcendental life – whereas even the Marcionite hoped for post-mortem felicity – then we shall make the best of our own phenomenal, and fabulous, world. But in so doing Diabolus loses all right to inveigh against the credulity and forgetfulness of religious believers. If God does not exist, why not deceive ourselves? Only the religious believer can think it obligatory to seek the truth, even the truth that God does *not* exist, just as it is only the religious believer that can denounce the world's injustice.

I end with a parable. We have woken, let us suppose, to find our-selves driving down a motor-way we did not build nor remember entering. At intervals we pass the wrecks of burnt-out cars and hear the screams of burning babies. We learn the costs to animals, to human families that must accompany the building and maintenance of such a road, all that we may achieve a temporary destination that much more speedily. There are not exits, only service stations, and our only escape (if any) is by death. What shall we do? Bury the risk, the knowledge of agony, in comfortable amnesia? Become an ambulance-driver till despair sets in? Fantasise some future felicity in which the dead, the maimed are 'casualties, fallen on the field of honour' (Teilhard de Chardin *Human Energy* p. 50)? Crash the barrier? It is hardly surprising that in comfortable times and classes amnesia is the preferred option. As that possibility grows more remote it will also not be surprising if the religious solution, in Gnostic or in Catholic form, comes to seem our salvation. 'Men are asleep, they awaken at their death'.[5] What other hope is there? What honest faith is possible without that hope?

NOTES

1. I am grateful to the Philosophical Society of the University of Stirling for criticism of an earlier draft.
2. See my *The Moral Status of Animals* (Oxford, 1977), pp. 42 ff. for an elaboration of this point.
3. *Free enquiry into the nature and origin of evil* (1757); see also Samuel Johnson's review in *Collected Works* (1787), vol. X, pp. 220 ff.
4. Ramchandra Gandhi has made a similar point in *The Availability of Religious Ideas*, pp. 49 f.
5. Attributed to Mohammed by Ibn Arabi: H. Gorbin, *Creative Imagination in the Sufism of Ibn Arabi*, p. 208.

Delivered at the Meeting of the Aristotelian Society at 5/7, Tavistock Place, London, W.C.1, on Monday 30th May 1977, at 7.30 p.m.

QUESTIONS for further discussion:

Granting Clark's contention (roughly) that the decision to trust our cognitive processes to tell us what is good and true, and therefore if we are consequent in our thinking, our decision for religion, cannot itself be *justified* by appeal to these processes, in what ways, if at all, might we justify the choice of the catholic as against the gnostic solution, or vice versa? If Clark's assumption (A) is confirmed that 'the world is not one that a decent Creator can easily be supposed to have created', and if the mind–body problem is best resolved by concluding that the mental and the physical are independent of each other, a Gnostic view will presumably be the better justified. If, however, mind somehow depends on matter, and if Clark's other suggestion (B) is adopted ('perhaps He [the Omniscient] must create in order to know what the world He creates is like, and having created should sustain it till it can achieve its own felicity') or no inconsistency between evil and God has been shown, as Plantinga holds, a catholic view will be better justified. Such preferences will be on grounds of rational consistency, rationality having been already chosen.

However, suppose A is confirmed but the mental is found to depend on the physical, or suppose that B, on consideration seems likely to be true, while mind and body can be shown to be independent of each other, what options are then open to us? Can we, for instance, choose to be *somewhat* rational? Or should we wait to see which propositions, A or B, or our view on the mind–body problem, comes to appear rationally most questionable?

Paper IX
Introductory Groundwork

Believing in God may in some contexts be a matter simply of believing that God exists, that there is a God. And, certainly, unless a person does believe that there is a God, it is hard to see in what his or her believing in God consists. Characteristically, however, believing in God also involves loving, trusting, and hoping in God. Again characteristically (if not essentially) it also involves praying to God, and in particular making requests of God. Yet this practice, the practice of petitionary prayer has seemed irrational not only to those who believe that no God exists, but precisely to those who believe in the existence of an omnipotent, omniscient and unfailingly loving God. In the following paper the argument is carefully articulated, and discussed. Informally put, the contention of the theistic person who doubts the rationality of petitionary prayer is that God will surely bring about the best world which it is within His power to bring about anyhow, without anyone's asking for it. Trust in God's loving omnicompetence may thus be argued to exclude petitionary prayer.

Petitionary Prayer

ELEONORE STUMP

Ordinary Christian believers of every period have in general taken prayer to be fundamentally a request made of God for something specific believed to be good by the one praying. The technical name for such prayer is 'impetration'; I am going to refer to it by the more familiar designation 'petitionary prayer.' There are, or course, many important kinds of prayer which are not requests; for example, most of what is sometimes called 'the higher sort of prayer' – praise, adoration, thanksgiving – does not consist in requests and is not included under petitionary prayer. But basic, common petitionary prayer poses problems that do not arise in connection with the more contemplative varieties of prayer, and it is petitionary prayer with its special problems that I want to examine in this paper.

Of those problems, the one that has perhaps been most discussed in the recent literature is the connection between petitionary prayer and miracles. For instance, if one believes in divine response to petitionary prayer, is one thereby committed to a belief in miracles? But as much as possible I want to avoid this issue (and several others involving petitionary prayer[1]) in order to concentrate on just one problem. It is, I think, the problem stemming from petitionary prayer which has most often occurred to ordinary Christian believers from the Patristic period to the present. Discussion of it can be found, for example, in Origen's third-century treatise on prayer,[2] in various writings of Aquinas,[3] and, very recently, in a book by Keith Ward.[4]

Put roughly and succinctly, the problem comes to this: is a belief in the efficacy and usefulness of petitionary prayer consistent with a belief in an omniscient, omnipotent, perfectly good God? It is, therefore, a problem only on certain assumptions drawn from an ordinary, orthodox, traditional view of God and of petitionary prayer. If one thinks, for example, as D. Z. Phillips does,[5] that all 'real' petitionary prayer is reducible to the petition 'Thy will be done,' then the problem I want to discuss evaporates. And if one thinks of God as the unknowable, non-denumerable, ultimate reality, which is not an entity at all, as Keith Ward does,[6] the problem I am interested in does not even arise. The cases which concern me in this paper are those in which someone praying a petitionary prayer makes a specific request freely (at least in his own view) of an omniscient, omnipotent, perfectly good God, conceived of in the traditional orthodox way. I am specifying that the prayers are made freely because I want to discuss this problem on the assumption that man has free will and that not everything is predetermined. I am making this assumption, first because I want to examine the problem of petitionary prayer as it arises for ordinary Christian believers, and I think their understanding of the problem typically includes the assumption that man has free will, and secondly because adopting the opposite view enormously complicates the attempt to understand and justify petitionary prayer. If all things are predetermined – and worse, if they are all predetermined by the omnipotent and omniscient God to whom one is praying – it is much harder to conceive of a satisfactory justification for petitionary prayer. One consequence of my making this assumption is that I will not be drawing on important traditional Protestant accounts of prayer such as those given by Calvin and Luther, for instance since while they may be thoughtful, interesting accounts, they assume God's complete determination of everything.

I think that I can most effectively and plausibly show the problem which interests me by presenting a sketchy analysis of the Lord's Prayer. It is a prayer attributed to Christ himself, who is supposed to have produced it just for the purpose of teaching his disciples how they ought to pray. So it is an example of prayer which orthodox Christians accept as a paradigm, and it is, furthermore, a clear instance of petitionary prayer. Consequently, it is a particularly good example for my purposes. In what follows, I want to make clear, I am not concerned either to take account of contemporary Biblical exegesis or to contribute to it. I want simply to have a look at the prayer – in fact, at only half the prayer – as it is heard and prayed by ordinary twentieth-century Christians.

As the prayer is given in Luke 11, it contains seven requests. The last four have to do with the personal needs of those praying, but the first three are requests of a broader sort.

The first, 'Hallowed be thy name,' is commonly taken as a request that God's name be regarded as holy.[7] I am not sure what it means to regard God's name as holy, and I want to avoid worries about the notion of having attitudes towards God's *name*. All the same, I think something of the following sort is a sensible interpretation of the request. The common Biblical notion of holiness has as its root a sense of strong separateness.[8] And it may be that to regard God's name as holy is only to react to it very differently from the way in which one reacts to any other name – and that could happen because it seems specially precious or also (for example) because it seems specially feared. On this understanding of the request, it would be fulfilled if everyone (or almost everyone) took a strongly emotional and respectful attitude towards God's name. But it may be that this is too complicated as an interpretation of the request, and that to regard God's name as holy is simply to love and revere it. In that case, the request is fulfilled if everyone or almost everyone regards God's name very reverentially. And there are New Testament passages which foretell states of affairs fulfilling both these interpretations of the request – prophesying a time at or near the end of the world when all men fear or love God's name, and a time when the inhabitants of earth are all dedicated followers of God.[9]

The second request in the Lord's Prayer is that God's kingdom come. Now according to orthodox Judaeo-Christian beliefs, God is and always has been ruler of the world. What then does it mean to ask for the advent of his kingdom? Plainly, there is at least some sense in which the kingdom of heaven has not yet been established on earth and can be waited and hoped for. And this request seems to be for those millennial times when everything on earth goes as it ought to go, when men beat their swords into plowshares (Is. 2:4) and the wolf dwells at peace with the lamb (Is. 11:6, 65:25). This too, then, is a request for a certain state of affairs involving all or most men, the state of affairs at the end of the world prophesied under one or another description in Old and New Testament passages (cf., e.g., Rev. 21:1-4).

And it seems closely related to the object of the third request, 'Thy will be done on earth as it is in heaven.' There is, of course, a sense in which, according to Christian doctrine, God's will is always done on earth. But that is the sense in which God allows things to happen as they do (God's so-called 'permissive will'). God permits certain people to have evil intentions, he permits certain people to commit crimes, and so on, so that he wills to let happen what does happen; and in this sense his will is always done. But in heaven, according to Christian doctrine, it is not that God permits what occurs to occur, and so wills in accordance with what happens, but rather that what happens happens in accordance with his will. So only the perfect good willed unconditionally by God is ever done in heaven. For God's will to be done on earth in such a way, everyone on earth would always have to do only good. This request, then, seems to be another way of asking for the establishment of God's kingdom on earth; and it also seems linked with certain New Testament prophecies – there will be a 'new earth,' and the righteous meek will inherit it (cf., e.g., Mt. 5:5 and Rev. 5:10 and 21:1-4).

What I think is most worth noticing in this context about all three of these first requests of the Lord's Prayer is that it seems absolutely pointless, futile, and absurd to make them. All three seem to be requests for the millennium or for God's full reign on earth. But it appears from New Testament prophecies that God has already determined to bring about such a state of affairs in the future. And if God has predetermined that there will be such a time, then what is asked for in those three requests is already sure to come. But, then, what is the point of making the prayer? Why ask for something that is certain to come whether you beg for it or flee from it? It is no answer to these questions to say, as some theologians have done,[10] that one prays in this way just because Jesus prescribed such a prayer. That attempt at an answer simply transfers responsibility for the futile action from the one praying to the one being prayed to; it says nothing about what sense there is in the prayer itself. On the other hand, if, contrary to theological appearances, the things prayed for are not predetermined and their occurence or nonoccurrence is still in doubt, *could* the issue possibly be resolved by someone's asking for one or another outcome? If Jimmy Carter, say, (or some other Christian) does not ask for God's kingdom to come, will God therefore fail to establish it? Or will he establish it *just because* Jimmy Carter asked for it, though he would not have done so otherwise? Even Carter's staunchest supporters might well find it frightening to think so; and yet if we do not answer these questions in the affirmative, the prayer seems futile and pointless. So either an omniscient, omnipotent, perfectly good God has predetermined this state of affairs or he hasn't; and either way, asking for it seems to make no sense. This conclusion is applicable to other cases of petitionary prayer as well. To take just one example, suppose that Jimmy Carter prays the altruistic and Christian prayer that a particular atheistic friend of his be converted and so saved from everlasting damnation. If it is in God's power to save that man, won't he do so without Jimmy Carter's prayers? Won't a perfectly good God do all the good he can no matter what anyone prays for or does not pray for? Consequently, either God of his goodness will save the man in any case, so that the prayer is pointless, or there is some point in the prayer but God's goodness appears impugned.

We can, I think, generalise these arguments to all petitionary prayer by means of a variation on the argument from evil against God's existence.[11] (The argument that follows does not seem to me to be an acceptable one, but it is the sort of argument that underlies the objections to petitionary prayer which I have been presenting. I will say something about what I think are the flaws in this argument later in the paper.)

(1) A perfectly good being never makes the world worse than it would otherwise be if he can avoid doing so.

The phrase 'than it would otherwise be' here should be construed as 'than the world would have been had he not brought about or omitted to bring about some state of affairs.' In other words, a perfectly good being never makes the world, in virtue of what he himself does or omits to do, worse than it would have been had he not done or omitted to do something or other. *Mutatis mutandis*, the same remarks apply to 'than it would otherwise be' in (4) and (7) below.

(2) An omniscient and omnipotent being can avoid doing anything which it is not logically necessary for him to do.

∴ (3) An omniscient, omnipotent, perfectly good being never makes the world worse than it would otherwise be unless it is logically necessary for him to do so. (1, 2)

(4) A perfectly good being always makes the world better than it would otherwise be if he can do so.

(5) An omniscient and omnipotent being can do anything which it is not logically impossible for him to do.

∴ (6) An omniscient, omnipotent, perfectly good being always makes the world better than it would otherwise be unless it is logically impossible for him to do so. (4, 5)

(7) It is never logically necessary for an omniscient, omnipotent, perfectly good being to make the world worse than it would otherwise be; it is never logically impossible for an

omniscient, omnipotent, perfectly good being to make the
world better than it would otherwise be.

∴ (8) An omniscient, omnipotent, perfectly good being never
makes the world worse than it would otherwise be and always
makes the world better than it would otherwise be. (3, 6, 7)

This subconclusion implies that unless the world is infinitely improvable, either the world is or will be absolutely perfect or there is no omniscient, omnipotent, perfectly good being. In other words, (8) with the addition of a pair of premises –

(i) The world is not infinitely improvable

and (ii) It is not the case that the world is or will be absolutely
perfect (i.e., there is and always will be evil in the world) –

implies the conclusion of the argument from evil. That is not a surprising result since this argument is dependent on the argument from evil.[12]

(9) What is requested in every petitionary prayer is or results in
a state of affairs the realisation of which would make the
world either worse or better than it would otherwise be
(that is, than it would have been had that state of affairs not
been realised).

It is not always clear whether a petitionary prayer is requesting just an earthly state of affairs, or God's bringing about that earthly state of affairs. So, for example, when a mother prays for the health of her sick son, it is not always clear whether she is requesting simply the health of her son or God's restoration of the health of her son. If we can determine the nature of the request on the basis of what the one praying desires and hopes to get by means of prayer, then at least in most cases the request will be just for some earthly state of affairs. What is important to the mother is simply her son's getting well. For a case in which the request is for God's bringing about some earthly state of affairs, we might consider Gideon's prayer concerning the fleece, discussed below. In any event, I intend 'state of affairs' in this argument to range broadly enough to cover both sorts of cases.

∴ (10) If what is requested in a petitionary prayer is or results in a
state of affairs the realisation of which would make the
world worse than it would otherwise be, an omniscient,
omnipotent, perfectly good being will not fulfil that
request. (8)

∴ (11) If what is requested in a petitionary prayer is or results in

a state of affairs the realisation of which would make the
world better than it would otherwise be, an omniscient,
omnipotent, perfectly good being will bring about that
state of affairs even if no prayer for its realisation has been
made. (8)

It might occur to someone here that what is requested in at least some
petitionary prayers is that God bring about a certain state of affairs *in
response to the particular petitionary prayer being made*. In such cases, of
course, it is logically impossible that God bring about what is requested in the petitionary prayer in the absence of that petitionary
prayer. It is not clear to me that there are such cases. The familiar
entreaties such as 'Hear the voice of my supplications' (Ps. 28:2) in the
Psalms seem to me not to be cases of the relevant sort, because they
seem to be an elaborate 'Please' rather than anything influencing the
nature of what is requested in the prayer. Perhaps one of the best
candidates for such a case is Gideon's prayer about the fleece: 'If you
will save Israel by my hand, as you have said, I will put a fleece of
wool on the floor and if the dew is on the fleece only and it is dry on
all the earth, then I will know that you will save Israel by my hand, as
you have said' (Judges 6:36–37; cf. also 6:39). Gideon here is requesting that God give him a sign by means of the fleece of wool. Does his
prayer amount to a request that God produce dew only on the fleece
and not on the surrounding ground, or does it come to a request that
God do so in response to Gideon's prayer? If there are cases in which
the request implicitly or explicitly includes reference to the prayer
itself, then in those cases the inference from (8) to (11) is not valid; and
such cases ought simply to be excluded from consideration in this
argument.

∴ (12) Petitionary prayer effects no change. (9, 10, 11)

There is, of course, a sense in which the offering of a prayer is itself a
new state of affairs and accompanies or results in natural, psychological changes in the one praying, but step (12) ought to be understood
as saying that no prayer is itself efficacious in causing a change of the
sort it was designed to cause. An argument which might be thought to
apply here, invalidating the inference to the conclusion (13), is that
prayer need not effect any change in order to be considered efficacious,
provided the offering of the prayer itself is a sufficient reason in God's
view for God's fulfilment of the prayer.[13] In other words, if, for certain
reasons apart from consideration of a prayer for a state of affairs S, God

has determined to bring about *S*, a prayer for *S* may still be considered to be efficacious if and only if God would have brought about *S* just in response to the prayer for *S*. But I think that even if this view is correct, it does not in fact invalidate the inference to (13). There is a difference between being efficacious and having a point. This argument about the efficacy of prayer 'seems to assume that not all answers to prayer will be of the overdetermined type. And as long as a believer is not in a position to know which states of affairs are divinely determined to occur regardless of prayers, there is some point in petitionary prayer – any given case may be one in which God would not have brought about the desired state of affairs without prayer for it. But if it is the case for every fulfilled prayer that God would have brought about the desired state of affairs without the prayer, it does seem that there is no point in petitionary prayer, except for those cases (which I think must at best form a very small minority) in which the real object of the one praying a petitionary prayer is not so much to see the realisation of the state of affairs he is requesting as to have some influence on or contact with the Deity by means of petitionary prayer; and such cases may then simply be excepted from the conclusion of the argument.

∴ (13) Petitionary prayer is pointless. (12)

The basic strategy of this argument is an attempt to show that there is an inconsistency between God's goodness and the efficacy of petitionary prayer; but it is possible to begin with other divine attributes and make a case for a similar inconsistency, so that we can have other, very different arguments to the same conclusion, namely that petitionary prayer is pointless. Perhaps the most formidable of such alternative arguments is the one based on God's immutability, an argument the strategy of which can be roughly summarised in this way. Before a certain petitionary prayer is made, it is the case either that God will bring about the state of affairs requested in the prayer or that he will not bring it about. He cannot have left the matter open since doing so would imply a subsequent change in him and he is immutable. Either way, since he is immutable, the prayer itself can effect no change in the state of affairs and hence is pointless. Even leaving aside problems of foreknowledge and free will to which this argument (or attempted objections to it) may give rise, I think that orthodox theology will find no real threat in the argument because of the doctrine of God's eternality. However problematic that doctrine may be in itself, it undercuts arguments such as this one because it maintains God's atemporality.[14] My thirteen-step argument against petitionary prayer is, then, not the only argument rejecting petitionary prayer on theistic principles, but it (or some argument along the same lines) does, I think, make the strongest case against petitionary prayer, given Christian doctrine.

The premiss that is most likely to appear false in the argument, at first reading, is (9) because one is inclined to think that there are many petitionary prayers which, if they are granted, would not make the world either better or worse than it would otherwise be. Such a view might be accommodated without damaging the argument simply by weakening (9) and the conclusion: many petitionary prayers, and surely the most important ones, are such that if fulfilled they make the world either a better or a worse place. But I think it is possible to argue plausibly for (9) in the strong form I have given it. Take, for instance, the case of a little boy who prays for a jack-knife. Here, we might think, we have an example of a petitionary prayer the fulfilment of which makes the world neither better nor worse. But, on the one hand, if the little boy has prayed for a jack-knife, surely he will be happier if he gets it, either because he very much wants a jack-knife or because God has honored his request. Consequently, one could argue that fulfilling the request makes the world better in virtue of making the one praying happier. Or, on the other hand, if we think of the little boy's prayer for a jack-knife from God's point of view, then we see that fulfilment of the prayer involves not just the little boy's acquiring a jack-knife but also God's bringing it about in answer to prayer that the little boy acquire a jack-knife. Fulfilling the prayer, then, will have an influence on at least the little boy's religious beliefs and perhaps also on those of his parents and even on those of the people in his parents' community. One might argue that the influence in this case would be deleterious (since it is conducive to wrong views of the purpose of prayer and of relationship with God), and consequently that fulfilling this prayer would make the world a worse place than it would otherwise be. So I think it is possible to argue plausibly that the fulfilment of even such a prayer would make the world either a worse or a better place.

Christian literature contains a number of discussions of the problem with petitionary prayer and various attempts to solve it. For the sake of brevity, I want to look just at the proposed solution Aquinas gives. It is the most philosophically sophisticated of the solutions I know; and in the wake of the twentieth-century revival of Thomism, it is the solution adopted by many theologians and theistic philosophers today.[15] Thomas discusses problems of petitionary prayer in his Sentence commentary and in *Summa contra gentiles*,[16] but the clearest expositions of his views is in the question on prayer in the *Summa theologiae*, where he devotes an entire article to showing that there is sense and usefulness in petitionary prayer.[17] The basic argument he relies on to rebut various objections against the usefulness of prayer is this. Divine Providence determines not only what effects there will be in the world, but also what causes will give rise to those effects and in what order they will do so. Now human actions, too, are causes. 'For,' Thomas says, 'we pray not in order to change the divine disposition but for the sake of acquiring by petitionary prayer what God has disposed to be achieved by prayer.'[18]

Perhaps the first worry which this argument occasions stems from the appearance of theological determinism in it: God determines not only what effects there will be but also what the causes of those effects will be and in what order the effects will be produced. It is hard to see how such a belief is compatible with freedom of the will. In the preamble to this argument, however, Thomas says he is concerned *not* to deny free will but, on the contrary, to give an account of prayer which preserves free will. So I want simply to assume that he has in mind some distinction or some theory which shows that, despite appearances, his argument is not committed to a thorough-going determinism, and I am going to ignore any troubles in the argument having to do with the compatibility of predestination or foreknowledge and free will.

For present purposes, what is more troublesome about this argument is that it does not provide any real help with the problem it means to solve. According to Thomas, there is nothing absurd or futile about praying to God, given God's nature, because God has by his providence arranged things so that free human actions and human prayers will form part of the chain of cause and effect leading to the state of the world ordained in God's plan. And so, on Thomas's view, prayer should not be thought of as an attempt to get God to do something which he would not otherwise do but rather as an effort to produce an appropriate and preordained cause which will result in certain effects since God in his providence has determined things to be so. Now surely there can be no doubt that, according to Christian doctrine, God wants men to pray and answers prayers; and consequently it is plain that God's plan for the world includes human prayers as causes of certain effects. The difficulty lies in explaining how such a doctrine makes sense. Why should prayers be included in God's plan as causes of certain effects? And what sense is there in the notion that a perfect and unchangeable God, who disposes and plans everything, fulfils men's prayers asking him to do one thing or another? Thomas's argument, I think, gives no help with these questions and so gives no help with this problem of petitionary prayer.

This argument of Thomas's is roughly similar in basic strategy to other traditional arguments for prayer[19] and is furthermore among the most fully developed and sophisticated arguments for prayer, but it seems to me inadequate to make sense of petitionary prayer. I think, then, that it is worthwhile exploring a sort of argument different from those that stress the connection between God's omniscience or providence and men's prayers. In what follows I want to offer a tentative and preliminary sketch of the way in which such an argument might go.

Judaeo-Christian concepts of God commonly represent God as loving mankind and wanting to be loved by men in return. Such anthropomorphic talk is in sharp contrast to the more sophisticated-sounding language of the Hellenised and scholastic arguments considered so far. But a certain sort of anthropomorphism is as much a part of Christianity as is Thomas's 'perfect being theology,'[20] and it, too, builds on intricate philosophical analysis, beginning perhaps with Boethius's attempt in *Contra Eutychen et Nestorium* to explain what it means to say of something that it is a person. So to say that God loves men and wants to be loved in return is to say something that has a place in philosophical theology and is indispensable to Christian doctrine. Throughout the Old and New Testaments, the type of loving relationship wanted between man and God is represented by various images, for example, sometimes as the relationship between husband and wife, sometimes as that between father and child. And sometimes (in the Gospel of John, for instance) it is also represented as the relationship between true friends.[21] But if the relationship between God and human beings is to be one which at least sometimes can be accurately represented as the love of true friendship, then there is a problem for both parties to the relationship, because plainly it will not be easy for there to be friendship between an omniscient, omnipotent, perfectly good person and a fallible, finite, imperfect person. The troubles of generating and maintaining friendship in such a case are surely the perfect paradigms of which the troubles of friendship between a Rockefeller child and a slum child are just pale copies. Whatever other troubles there are for friendship in these cases, there are at least two dangers for the disadvantaged or inferior member of the pair. First, he can be so overcome by the advantages or superiority of his 'friend' that he becomes simply a shadowy reflection of the other's personality, a slavish follower who slowly loses all sense of his own tastes and desires and will. Some people, of course believe that just this sort of attitude towards God is what Christianity wants and gets from the best of its adherents; but I think that such a belief goes counter to the spirit of the Gospels, for example, and I don't think that it can be found even in such intense mystics as St. Teresa and St. John of the Cross. Secondly, in addition to the danger of becoming completely dominated, there is the danger of becoming spoiled in the way that members of a royal family in a ruling house are subject to. Because of the power at their disposal in virtue of their connections, they often become tyrannical, willful, indolent, self-indulgent, and the like. The greater the discrepancy in status and condition between the two friends, the greater the danger of even inadvertently overwhelming and oppressing or overwhelming and spoiling the lesser member of the pair; and if he is overwhelmed in either of these ways, the result will be replacement of whatever kind of friendship there might have been with one or another sort of using. Either the superior member of the pair will use the lesser as his lackey, or the lesser will use the superior as his personal power source. To put it succinctly, then, if god wants some kind of true friendship with men, he will have to find a way of guarding against both kinds of overwhelming.

It might occur to someone to think that even if we assume the view that God wants friendship between himself and human beings, it does not follow that he will have any of the problems just sketched, because he is omnipotent.[22] If he wants friendship of this sort with men, one might suppose, let him just will it and it will be his. I do not want to stop here to argue against this view in detail, but I do want just to suggest that there is reason for thinking it to be incoherent, at least on the assumption of free will adopted at the beginning of this paper, because it is hard to see how God could bring about such a friendship magically, by means of his omnipotence, and yet permit the people involved to have free will. If he could do so, he could make a person freely love him in the right sort of way, and it does not seem reasonable to think he could do so.[23] On the face of it, then, omnipotence alone does not do away with the two dangers for friendship that I sketched above. But the institution of petitionary prayer, I think, can be understood as a safeguard against these dangers.

It is easiest to argue that petitionary prayer serves such a function in the case of a man who prays for himself. In praying for himself, he makes an explicit request for help, and he thereby acknowledges a need or a desire and his dependence on God for satisfying that need or desire. If he gets what he prayed for, he will be in a position to attribute his good fortune to God's doing and to be grateful to God for what God has given him. If we add the undeniable uncertainty of his getting what he prays for, then we will have safeguards against what I will call (for lack of a better phrase) overwhelming spoiling. These conditions make the act of asking a safeguard against tyrannical and self-indulgent pride, even if the one praying thinks of himself grandly as having God on his side.

We can see how the asking guards against the second danger, of oppressive overwhelming, if we look for a moment at the function of roughly similar asking for help when both the one asking and the one asked are human beings. Suppose a teacher sees that one of his students is avoiding writing a paper and is thereby storing up trouble for himself at the end of the term. And suppose that the student *asks* the teacher for extra help in organising working time and scheduling the various parts of the work. In that case I think the teacher can without any problem give the student what he needs, provided, of course, that the teacher is willing to do as much for any other student and so on. But suppose, on the other hand, that the student does not ask the teacher for help and that the teacher instead calls the student at home and simply presents him with the help he needs in scheduling and discipline. The teacher's proposals in that case are more than likely to strike the student as meddling interference, and he is likely to respond with more or less polite variations on 'Who asked you?' and 'Mind your own business.' These responses, I think, are healthy and just. If the student were having ordinary difficulties getting his work done and yet docilely and submissively accepted the teacher's unrequested scheduling of his time, he would have taken the first step in the direction of unhealthly passivity towards his teacher. And if he and his teacher developed that sort of relationship, he could end by becoming a lackey-like reflection of his teacher. Bestowing at least some benefits only in response to requests for them is a safeguard against such an outcome when the members of the relationship are not equally balanced.

It becomes much harder to argue for this defense of prayer as soon as the complexity of the case is increased even just a little. Take, for example, Monica's praying for her son Augustine. There is nothing in Monica's praying for Augustine which shows that *Augustine* recognises that he has a need for God's help or that *he* will be grateful if God gives him what *Monica* prays for. Nor is it plain that *Monica's* asking shields Augustine from oppressive overwhelming by God. So it seems as if the previous arguments fail in this case. But consider again the case in which a teacher sees that a student of his could use help but does not feel that he can legitimately volunteer his help unasked. Suppose that John, a friend of that student, comes to see the teacher and says, 'I don't know if you've noticed, but Jim is having trouble getting to his term paper. And unless he gets help, I think he won't do it at all and will be in danger of flunking the course.' If the teacher now goes to help Jim and is rudely or politely asked 'What right have you to interfere?' he'll say, 'Well, in fact, your friend came to me and *asked* me to help.' And if John is asked the same question, he will probably reply, 'But I'm your friend; I had to do *something*.' I think, then, that because John asks the teacher, the teacher is in a position to help with less risk of oppressive meddling than before. Obviously, he cannot go very far without incurring that risk as fully as before; and perhaps the most he can do if he wants to avoid oppressive meddling is to try to elicit from *Jim* in genuinely uncoercive ways a request for help. And, of course, I chose Monica and Augustine to introduce this case because, as Augustine tells it in the *Confessions*, God responded to Monica's fervent and continued prayers for Augustine's salvation by arranging the circumstances of Augustine's life in such a way that finally Augustine himself freely asked God for salvation.

One might perhaps think that there is something superfluous and absurd in God's working through the intermediary of prayer in this way. If Jim's friend can justify his interference on the grounds that he is Jim's friend and has to do *something*, God can dispense with this sort of petitionary prayer, too. He can give aid unasked on the grounds that he is the *creator* and has to do something. But suppose that Jim and John are only acquaintances who have discussed nothing more than their schoolwork; and suppose that John, by overhearing Jim's phone conversations, has come to believe that all Jim's academic troubles are just symptoms of problems he is having with his parents. If John asks the teacher to help Jim with his personal problems, and if the teacher begins even a delicate attempt to do so by saying that John asked him to do so, he and John could properly be told to mind their own business. It is not the *status* of his relationship or even the depth of his care and compassion for Jim which puts John in a position to defend himself by saying 'But I'm your friend.' What protects John against the charge of oppressive meddling is rather the degree to which Jim has freely, willingly, shared his life and thoughts and feelings with John. So John's line of defense against the charge of oppressive meddling can be attributed to God only if the person God is to aid has willingly shared his thoughts and feelings and the like with God. But it is hard to imagine anyone putting himself in such a relation to a person he believes to be omnipotent and good without his also *asking* for whatever help he needs.

Even if the argument can be made out so far, one might be inclined to think that it will not be sufficient to show the compatibility of God's goodness with the practice of petitionary prayer. If one supposes that God brought Augustine to Christianity in response to Monica's prayers, what is one to say about Augustine's fate if Monica had not prayed for him? And what does this view commit one to maintain about people who neither pray for themselves nor are prayed for? It looks as if an orthodox Christian who accepts the argument about petitionary prayer so far will be committed to a picture of this sort. God is analogous to a human father with two very different children. Both Old and New Testaments depict God as doing many good things for men without being asked to do so, and this human father, too, does unrequested good things for both his children. But one child, who is healthy and normal, with healthy, normal relations to his father, makes frequent requests of the father which the father responds to and in virtue of which he bestows benefits on the child. The other child is selectively blind, deaf, dumb, and suffering from whatever other maladies are necessary to make it plausible that he does not even know he has a father. Now either there are some benefits that the father will never bestow unless and until he is asked; and in that case he will do less for his defective child, who surely has more need of his help than does the healthy child. Or, on the other hand, he will bestow all his benefits unasked on the defective child, and then he seems to make a mockery of his practice with the normal child of bestowing some benefits only in response to requests – he is, after all, willing to bestow the same benefits without being asked. So it seems that we are still left with the problem we started with: either God is not perfectly good or the practice of petitionary prayer is pointless. But suppose the father always meets the defective child's needs and desires even though the child never comes to know of the existence of his father. The child knows only that he is always taken care of, and when he needs something, he gets what he needs. It seems to me intuitively clear that such a practice runs a great risk, at least, of making the defective child willful and tyrannical. But even if the defective child is not in danger of being made worse in some respects in this situation, still it seems plain that he would be better off if the father could manage to put the child in a position to know his father and to frame a request for what he wants. So I think a good father will fulfill the child's needs unasked; but I think that he can do so without making a mockery of his practice of bestowing benefits in response to requests only if putting the child in a position to make requests is among his first concerns.

And as for the question whether God would have saved Augustine without Monica's prayers, I think that there is intermediate ground between the assertion that Monica's prayers are necessary to Augustine's salvation, which seems to impugn God's goodness, and the claim that they are altogether without effect, which undercuts petitionary prayer. It is possible, for example, to argue that God would have saved Augustine without Monica's prayers but not in the same amount of time or not by the same process or not with the same effect. Augustine, for instance, might have been converted to Christianity but not in such a way as to become one of its most powerful authorities for centuries.[24]

With all this, I have still looked only at cases that are easy for my position; when we turn to something like a prayer for Guatemala after the earthquake – which begins to come closer to the sort of petitions in the first half of the Lord's Prayer – it is much harder to know what to say. And perhaps it is simply too hard to come up with a

146

reasonable solution here because we need more work on the problem of evil. Why would a good God permit the occurrence of earthquakes in the first place? Do the reasons for his permitting the earthquake affect his afterwards helping the country involved? Our inclination is surely to say that a good God must *in any case* help the earthquake victims, so that in this instance at any rate it is pointless to pray. But plainly we also have strong inclinations to say that a good God must in any case prevent earthquakes in populated areas. And since orthodox Christianity is committed to distrusting these latter inclinations, it is at least at sea about the former ones. Without more work on the problem of evil, it is hard to know what to say about the difference prayer might make in this sort of case.

I think it is worth noticing, though, that the first three requests of the Lord's prayer do not run into the same difficulties. Those requests seem generally equivalent to a request for the kingdom of God on earth, that state of affairs in which, of their own free will, all men on earth are dedicated, righteous lovers of God. Now suppose it is true that God would bring about his kingdom on earth if an individual Christian such as Jimmy Carter did not pray for it. It does not follow in this case, however, that the prayer in question is pointless and makes no difference. Suppose no one prayed for the advent of God's kingdom on earth or felt a need or desire for those millenial times strongly enough to pray for them. It seems unreasonable to think that God could bring about his earthly kingdom under those conditions, or if he could, that it would be the state of affairs just described, in which earth is populated by people who *freely* love God.[23] And if so, then making the requests in the first half of the Lord's Prayer resembles other, more ordinary activities in which only the effort of a whole group is sufficient to achieve the desired result. One man can't put out a forest fire, but if everyone in the vicinity of a forest fire realised that fact and on that basis decided not to try, the fire would rage out of control. So in the case of the opening petitions of the Lord's Prayer, too, it seems possible to justify petitionary prayer without impugning God's goodness.

Obviously, the account I have given is just a preliminary sketch for the full development of this solution, and a good deal more work needs to be done on the problem. Nonetheless, I think that this account is on the right track and that there is a workable solution to the problem of petitionary prayer which can be summarised in this way.

God must work through the intermediary of prayer, rather than doing everything on his own initiative, for man's sake. Prayer acts as a kind of buffer between man and God. By safeguarding the weaker member of the relation from the dangers of overwhelming domination and overwhelming spoiling, it helps to promote and preserve a close relationship between an omniscient, omnipotent, perfectly good person and a fallible, finite, imperfect person. There is, of course, something counter-intuitive in this notion that prayer acts as a buffer; prayer of all sorts is commonly and I think correctly said to have as one of its main functions the production of closeness between man and God. But not just any sort of closeness will result in friendship, and promoting the appropriate sort of closeness will require inhibiting or preventing inappropriate sorts of closeness, so that a relationship of friendship depends on the maintenance of both closeness and distance between the two friends. And while I do not mean to denigrate the importance of prayer in producing and preserving the appropriate sort of closeness, I think the problem of petitionary prayer at issue here is best solved by focusing on the distance necessary for friendship and the function of petitionary prayer in maintaining that distance.

As for the argument against prayer which I laid out at the start of the paper, it seems to me that the flaw lies in step (7), that it is never logically necessary for God to make the world worse than it would otherwise be and never logically impossible for him to make the world better than it would otherwise be. To take a specific example from among those discussed so far, orthodox Christianity is committed to claiming that the advent of God's kingdom on earth, in which all people freely love God, would make the world better than it would otherwise be. But I think that it is not possible for God to *make* the world better in this way, because I think it is not possible for him to *make* men *freely* do anything.[23] And in general, if it is arguable that God's doing good things just in virtue of men's requests protects men from the dangers described and preserves them in the right relationship to God, then it is not the case that it is always logically possible for God to make the world better and never logically necessary for him to make the world worse than it would otherwise be. If men do not always pray for all the good things they might and ought to pray for, then in some cases either God will not bring about some good thing or he will do so but at the expense of the good wrought and preserved by petitionary prayer.

It should be plain that there is nothing in this analysis of prayer which *requires* that God fulfil every prayer; asking God for something is not in itself a sufficient condition for God's doing what he is asked. Christian writings are full of examples of prayers which are not answered, and there are painful cases of unanswered prayer in which the one praying must be tempted more to the belief that God is his implacable enemy than to the sentimental-seeming belief that God is his friend. This paper proposes no answer for these difficulties. They require a long, hard, careful look at the problem of evil, and that falls just outside the scope of this paper.

And, finally, it may occur to someone to wonder whether the picture of God presented in this analysis is at all faithful to the God of the Old or New Testaments. Is this understanding of God and prayer anything that Christianity ought to accept or even find congenial? It seems to me that one could point to many stories in either the Old or New Testament in support of an affirmative answer – for example, Elijah's performance on Mt. Carmel (I Kings 18), or the apostles' prayer for a successor to Judas (Acts 1:24-26). But for a small and particularly nice piece of evidence, we can turn to the story in the Gospel of Luke which describes Jesus making the Lord's Prayer and giving a lecture on how one is to pray. According to the Gospel, Jesus is praying and in such a way that his disciples see him and know that he is praying. One of them makes a request of him which has just a touch of rebuke in it: teach us to pray, as *John* taught *his* disciples to pray (Lk. 11:1). If there is a note of rebuke there, it seems just. A religious master should teach his disciples to pray, and a good teacher does not wait until he is asked to teach his students important lessons. But Jesus is portrayed as a good teacher of just this sort in the Gospel of Luke.[25] Does the Gospel, then, mean its readers to understand that Jesus would not have taught his disciples how to pray if they had not requested it? And if it does not, why is Jesus portrayed as waiting until he is asked? Perhaps the Gospel means us to understand[26] that Jesus does so just in order to teach by experience as well as by sermon what is implicit throughout the Lord's Prayer: that asking makes a difference.[27]

NOTES

1. For a good recent account of the problem of petitionary prayer and miracles, see Robert Young, 'Petitioning God,' *American Philosophical Quarterly*, vol. 11 (1974), pp. 193-201. Other issues I intend to avoid include Peter Geach's worries about prayer

for events in the past in *God and the Soul* (London, 1969), pp. 89 ff., and about 'certain tensed propositions about the divine will . . . in connexion with prayer' (*op. cit.,* p. 97).

2. Eric George Jay, *Origen's Treatise on Prayer* (London, 1954), vols. V-VI, pp. 92-103.

3. Most notably, *Summa theologiae,* 2a-2ae, 83, 1-17; *Summa contra gentiles,* I.III. 95-96; *In IV. Sent.,* dist. XV, q. 4, a. 1.

4. *The Concept of God* (New York, 1974), pp. 221-222. Ward introduces the problem only as an embarrassment for what he calls 'Thomistic' theology. *Cf.* my review in *The Philosophical Review,* vol. 86 (1977), pp. 398-404.

5. *The Concept of Prayer* (New York, 1966), pp. 112 ff.

6. *Cf. The Concept of God (op. cit.)* pp. 62, 101, 111 and 185.

7. *Cf.,* for example, the similar understanding of this petition in two very different theologians: Augustine, *Homilies on the Gospels,* Serm. 6; and Calvin, *Institutes of the Christian Religion,* III. xx. 41.

8. The most common Old Testament word for 'holy' and its correlates is some form of '*kādash*,' the basic, literal meaning of which is separation, withdrawal, or state of being set apart; *cf.* Gesenius, *A Hebrew and English Lexicon of the Old Testament.* In the New Testament, the most frequently used word is '*hagiazō*' and its correlates, the basic meaning of which also includes the notion of being separate and being set apart; *cf.* Thayer, *A Greek-English Lexicon of the New Testament,* and Arndt and Gringich, *A Greek-English Lexicon of the New Testament and Other Early Christian Literature.*

9. *Cf.,* e.g., Is. 2: 2-21, 45: 23, and 65: 23; Matt. 24; Mk. 13; Lk. 21; and Rev. 6: 15-17.

10. See, for example, Martin Luther, *Large Catechism* pt. III. 169. Luther's argument for prayer has more force in the context of the catechism than it does in the context of a philosophical discussion, because Luther's purpose there is the practical one of blocking what he understands as believers' *excuses* for not praying.

11. My approach to the argument from evil, which underlies the following argument, owes a good deal to Carl Ginet and Norman Kretzmann.

12. There is a noteworthy difference between (ii) and the premiss ordinarily supplied in its stead in arguments from evil, namely, (ii') 'There is evil in the world'. The difference suggests a way to develop an alternative or at least an addition to the standard free will defense against the argument from evil.

13. See Terence Penelhum, *Religion and Rationality* (New York, 1971), pp. 287-292.

14. Norman Kretzmann and I examine the concept of eternity in ancient and medieval metaphysics and theology in our forthcoming book on that subject, attending particularly to the usefulness of the concept in resolving certain problems in rational theology.

15. See, for example, the articles on prayer in the *Dictionnaire de Théologie Catholique* and *The New Catholic Encyclopedia.*

16. See *In IV. Sent.,* dist. XV, q.4, a.l, and *Summa contra gentiles,* I. III. 95-96.

17. See 2a-2ae, q. 83, a.2.

18. See reply, a.2. '*Non enim propter hoc oramus ut divinam dispositionem immutemus: sed ut id impetremus quod Deus disposuit per orationes sanctorum implendum . . .*'

19. *Cf.*, e.g., Origen, *op. cit.*, and Augustine, *City of God*, Bk. V, ix.

20. Plainly, a good deal of skilful work is needed to weave such anthropomorphism and scholastic theology into one harmonious whole. The problem is, of course, given lengthy, detailed treatment in various scholastic writings, including Thomas's *Summa theologiae*.

21. See especially Jn. 15: 12-15.

22. I want to avoid detailed discussions of the various controversies over omnipotence. For present purposes, I will take this as a rough definition of omnipotence: a being is omnipotent if and only if he can do anything which is not logically impossible for him to do and if he can avoid doing anything which it is not logically necessary for him to do.

23. Controversy over this point is related to the more general controversy over whether or not it is possible for an omnipotent, omniscient, perfectly good God to create men who would on every occasion freely do what is right. For a discussion of that general controversy and arguments that it is not possible for God to do so, see Alvin Plantinga's *God and Other Minds* (Ithaca, 1967), pp. 132-148; I am in agreement with the general tenor of Plantinga's remarks in that section of his book.

24. I have presented the case of Monica and Augustine in a simplified form in order to have an uncomplicated hard case for the view I am arguing. As far as the historical figures themselves are concerned, it is plain that Monica's overt, explicit, passionate concern for her son's conversion greatly influenced the course of his life and shaped his character from boyhood on. It is not clear whether Augustine would have been anything like the man he was if his mother had not been as zealous on behalf of his soul as she was, if she had not prayed continually and fervently for his salvation and let him know she was doing so. Augustine's character and personality were what they were in large part as a result of her fierce desire for his espousal of Christianity; and just his knowledge that his beloved mother prayed so earnestly for his conversion must have been a powerful natural force helping to effect that conversion. In this context the question whether God could have saved Augustine without Monica's prayers takes on different meaning, and an affirmative answer is much harder to give with reasoned confidence.

25. See, for example, the lessons taught in the two incidents described in Lk. 21: 1-6.

26. I have used awkward circumlocutions in this paragraph in order to make plain that it is not my intention here to make any claims about the historical Jesus or the intentions of the Gospel writer. I am not concerned in this paper to do so or to take account of contemporary theories of Biblical exegesis. My point is only that the story in the Gospel, as it has been part of ordinary Christian tradition, lends itself to the interpretation I suggest.

27. In writing this paper, I have benefited from the comments and criticisms of John Boler, Norman Care, and Bill Rowe. I am particularly indebted to my friend Norman Kretzmann for his thorough reading and very helpful criticism of the paper. And I am grateful to John Crossett, from whom I have learned a great deal and whose understanding of philosophical problems in Christian theology is much better than my own.

QUESTIONS for further discussion:

If the institution of petitionary prayer may be the best or only way of seeing a relationship between God and His people by which His people are not overwhelmed or spoiled, then God's setting up such relationship as has petitionary prayer as an important mode, will be understandable. So, at least, runs the argument of the essay. However this argument will be undercut if there are *other* ways by which the relationship might as well or better have been secured against those dangers but *without* God's having to leave good things undone because these good things have not been requested. Are there such other ways? And does petitionary prayer as Christians and others envisage it carry with it disadvantages for the relationship which God is supposed to value?

FURTHER READING

One important consideration affecting the selection of readings in this book is that it can serve to introduce the reader to some of the most valuable recent writing in the Philosophy of Religion by republishing important contributions by leading authors in the field, to whose work the reader has thus gained some access. A most desirable, more substantial, further acquaintance can be had by consulting, in particular, the following:

Richard Swinburne, *The Existence of God*, Oxford University Press, London and New York, 1979.

Antony Flew, *The Presumption of Atheism*, Elek/Pemberton, London, 1976.

William L. Rowe, *The Cosmological Argument*, Princeton University Press, Princeton and London, 1975.

William J. Wainwright, *Mysticism*, Harvester, Brighton, 1981.

Stephen R. L. Clark, *The Lack of Gap between Fact and Value*, Proceedings of the Aristotelian Society, Supplementary Volume, 1980; *God's Law and Morality*, an article in the Journal, *Philosophical Quarterly*, for 1982.

The first two volumes, those by Swinburne and Flew, contain many further references to helpful reading. Less immediately relevant to the papers in the present collection but worthy of attention are Swinburne's

The Coherence of Theism, 1977, and

Faith and Reason, 1981, both published by Oxford University Press, London and New York, and

Flew (editor with A. MacIntyre), *New Essays in Philosophical Theology*, S.C.M. Press, London, 1955, essays whose chief preoccupation is with the meaningfulness of religious language, and *God and Philosophy*, Hutchinson, London, 1966.

Books providing introductory discussion, or discussion which calls for no previous engagement with the subject, include:

Anders Jeffner, *Butler and Hume on Religion*, Aktiebolaget Tryckmans, Stockholm, 1966.

Thomas MacPherson, *Philosophy and Religious Belief*, Hutchinson, London, 1974. A wide-ranging penetrating introduction to the field.

Basil Mitchell (editor), *Faith and Logic*, Allen & Unwin, London, 1955. These papers address largely the same questions as the Flew & MacIntyre, *New Essays*, listed above.

George I. Mavrodes (editor), *The Rationality of Belief in God*, Prentice Hall, Englewood Cliffs, N.J., 1970. These are the *loci classici* for historically important contentions in philosophical theology.

C. F. Delaney (editor), *Rationality and Religious Belief*, University of Notre Dame Press, Indiana & London, 1979. A number of very recent papers.

Kai Nielsen, *Contemporary Critiques of Religion*, Macmillan, London, 1971. Nielsen sides rather with the Critiques than with the Religion.

Terence Penelhum, *Problems of Religious Knowledge*, Macmillan, London, 1971, and

Basil Mitchell, *The Justification of Religious Belief*, Macmillan, London, 1973 are concerned with the epistemology of religious affirmations.

W. Donald Hudson, *A Philosophical Approach to Religion*, Macmillan, London, 1974. A relatively clear exposition of an approach which claims Wittgenstein as its inspiration.

Brian Davies, *An Introduction to the Philosophy of Religion*, Oxford, 1982.

Some topics are alluded to in passing in the course of this book; it will be useful to indicate where these are more fully explored.

The topic of the meaningfulness of religious language is of central concern in the collections listed above, edited by Flew & MacIntyre, and by Mitchell. For further discussion see:

William P. Alston, *Philosophy of Language*, Prentice Hall, Englewood Cliffs, N.J., 1964 (Chapter 4, especially), and

Alvin Plantinga, *God and Other Minds*, Cornell University Press, Ithaca and London, 1967 (Chapter 7, especially).

For a reply to Plantinga, see Nielsen, cited above.

The Ontological argument is well discussed in

Jonathan Barnes, *The Ontological Argument*, Macmillan, London, 1972.

Alvin Plantinga, *God, Freedom and Evil*, Allen and Unwin, London, 1975.

The justification of inductive argument is discussed in

Richard Swinburne (editor), *The Justification of Induction*, Oxford University Press, London and New York, 1974.

The Mind/Body relationship is discussed in

Keith Campbell, *Body and Mind*, Doubleday, Anchor Books, N.Y., 1970, and University of Notre Dame Press, 1980.

Richard Taylor, *Metaphysics*, Chapters 2, 3 and 4, Prentice Hall, Englewood Cliffs, N.J., 2nd Edition, 1974.

Passing now to matters discussed at some length in the body of the book, the notes frequently give help and guidance. The following will also repay study:

On Religious Experience and what is claimed for it:

Ronald W. Hepburn, *Christianity and Paradox* (Chapters called 'Encounters'), Watts, London, 1958.

Sidney Hook (Editor), *Religious Experience and Truth*, Oliver and Boyd, Edinburgh, 1962.

Steven T. Katz (Editor), *Mysticism and Philosophical Analysis*, Sheldon Press, London, 1978.

On Cosmological and Design Arguments:

Bertrand Russell, *Why I am not a Christian* (Chapters 1 and 13), e.g. Allen & Unwin, London, 1975.

R. W. Hepburn, cited above.

A. Plantinga, *God and Other Minds*, (Chapters 1 and 4).

A. Flew, *God and Philosophy*, cited above.

Anthony Kenny, *The Five Ways*, Routledge and Kegan Paul, London, 1969.

Richard Taylor, *Metaphysics*, Chapter 10, Prentice Hall, Englewood Cliffs, N.J., 2nd Edition, 1974.

On the Problem of Evil, see references to Hick and Plantinga in Introduction to Paper VIII.

On Morality and God's Will: Paul Helm (editor) *Divine Commands and Morality*, Oxford University Press, London and New York, 1981.

On whether one can consistently be a rational atheist:

C. S. Lewis, *Miracles*, Chapter III, Bles, London, 1947.

G. E. M. Anscombe, A Reply to Mr C. S. Lewis' Argument that 'Naturalism' is Self Refuting. In Professor Anscombe's *Collected Philosophical Papers*, Volume II, Blackwell, Oxford, 1981.

On Petitionary Prayer:

Peter T. Geach, *God and the Soul* (Chapter 7), Routledge and Kegan Paul, London, 1969.

INDEX

Index